BREWED IN THE PACIFIC NORTHWEST

Brewed in the Pacific Northwest

A History of Beer-Making in Oregon and Washington

by Gary and Gloria Meier

WESTERN WRITERS SERIES NO. 3

Fjord Press
Seattle
1991

We dedicate this book to the memory of
the Pacific Northwest pioneer brewers,
whose goal in life was to brew a good glass of beer.

Published and distributed by
Fjord Press
P.O. Box 16501
Seattle, Washington 98116
(206) 625-9363

Editors: Steven T. Murray & Tiina Nunnally
Cover design: Jane Fleming
Book design: Steven T. Murray
Typesetting: Nete Leth, Fjord Press
Printed on acid-free paper by Thomson-Shore

Library of Congress Cataloging-in-Publication Data

Meier, Gary.
Brewed in the Pacific Northwest : a history of beer-making
in Oregon and Washington / by Gary and Gloria Meier.
p. cm. — (Western writers series ; no. 3)
Includes bibliographical references and index.
ISBN 0-940242-54-0 (cloth) : $25.95 —
ISBN 0-940242-53-2 (trade paper) : $12.95
1. Breweries—Oregon. 2. Breweries—Washington (State)
I. Meier, Gloria. II. Title. III. Series: Western writers series
(Seattle, Wash.) ; no. 3.
TP573.U5M45 1991
338.7'6633'09795—dc20 91-23402

Printed in the United States of America
First edition, July 1991
Second printing, September 1991

Contents

"If you want a glass or keg of lager beer
to drive away the blues, go to Wetterer's brewery.
His brew cannot be beat."

Jacksonville *Oregon Sentinel*
October 10, 1863

Foreword

THE COMMERCIAL PRODUCTION of beer in the Pacific Northwest has a colorful tradition dating from 1852, when the first brewery was established in Portland. A succession of pioneer brewers followed with their own beer plants in other communities until, in the later decades of the 19th century, a great many Northwest cities, mining towns, logging settlements, and farming centers had breweries that proudly proclaimed their local product.

The familiar image of the old-time brewer as a jolly, rosy-cheeked, German-speaking, often portly gentleman, happily working away among his kettles and tubs and barrels, is nowhere more historically accurate than in the Pacific Northwest. They were predominantly German: adventurous Old World master brewers hoping for a better life in America. Welcomed early to the Pacific Northwest by a demand for good beer, the *Bräumeisters* were a special kind of pioneer. Arriving by wagon train or sailing ship, often with little more than a few clothes and a copper brewing kettle, they were ready to offer their time-honored art to a thirsty frontier.

Researching for this book was pleasant work for two history devotees who appreciate a good glass of beer. The information gleaned from old business records, directories, U.S. Brewers' Association archives, and early newspapers was interesting and often surprising. Did you know, for example, that Portland has hosted 21 active breweries over the years? Or that Spokane had eleven major brewing plants? Or that Pendleton had four? Washington's Port Angeles, Port Orchard, and Port Townsend all had breweries. Bellingham, Medford, and Eugene each had two, as did the little desert town of Burns in eastern Oregon.

There have been 138 breweries in Washington and 126 in Oregon. With three notable exceptions, all of the old-time breweries have vanished. Their distinctive bottles and labels are either nonexistent now or rare reminders of an earlier time. All of the breweries are listed in this book, along with stories and profiles of the brewers.

We are indebted to many brewing experts and historians for their assistance during our three years of research on the old breweries of Oregon and Washington. Of particular help were the friendly, patient, and knowledgeable staffs at Rainier, Olympia, and Blitz-Weinhard brewing companies, as well as the ladies and gentlemen at the Oregon Historical Society and the Washington State Historical Society.

We also wish to thank the folks at the many regional historical societies and museums in Washington and Oregon for their time and effort in looking through files and records to come up with answers to questions and little-known pieces of Northwest brewing history. You meet some of the nicest people in this kind of work.

Finally, we would like to thank Ray Jordan, friend and world-class bartender, for planting the seed of interest in us on a lazy afternoon some years ago, when he said: "Did you know that there were two big breweries right here in Eugene a long time ago?" We didn't.

This is the story of beer in Oregon and Washington.

Gary & Gloria Meier
Eugene, Oregon
April 1991

BREWED IN THE PACIFIC NORTHWEST

Chapter One

The Universal Beverage

AROUND 10,000 YEARS AGO, prehistoric humans in Asia made the accidental discovery that wild wheat and barley soaked in water to make gruel did not spoil when left out in the open air. Instead, natural yeast in the air converted it to a dark bubbling brew, and whoever drank it felt good.

From that time to this, almost every age, culture, and country in the world has made some kind of beer. Records from Mesopotamia show that beer was brewed there 7,000 years ago, and women were the master brewers of the day.

According to Egyptologist John Romer, ancient Egyptians brewed 70 kinds of beer called *hek,* and offered it as wages, along with bread and onions, to villagers for their work on the tombs of the Pharaohs. Priests made a special beer for celebrations as offerings to the gods, and during the rites the priests drank the beer.

Babylonians brewed their *bousa* from grain at least 2,200 years before Christ. A Babylonian seal thousands of years old, showing beer being made, is in New York's Metropolitan Museum of Art. The early Chinese made their beer from rice and called it *samshu,* and an Assyrian clay tablet relates that beer was taken aboard Noah's Ark. Even Julius Caesar is reported to have toasted his officers with beer in 49 B.C. after crossing the Rubicon River during his march on Rome.

The term "beer" did not come into common use until the Celtic word *beor* was applied to the malt brew produced in the monasteries of northern Gaul. It is thought that hops, which have a preservative and aromatic effect on beer, were first used by Gallic monks.

Through the Middle Ages, until about 1500, the production of beer was largely identified with churchmen. Each monastery had a brewhouse, and beer was closely associated with many religious and social celebrations. In fact, the word "bridal" comes from the Middle English *bride-ale* (and Scandinavian *brudöl*), a custom in which the bride poured ale for the wedding guests, who in turn presented gifts.

Beer in North America

When Columbus discovered the New World he found the natives of the West Indies enjoying a beerlike concoction. The great explorer noted that the brew was "a sort of wine, made of maize, resembling English beer." The Spanish conquistadors, who accompanied Cortez to Mexico in 1518 and then moved north to Navajo country in the present southwestern United States, found the natives drinking *chica,* a beer made from maize.

There is a historical record of domestic brewing—the first by colonists in North America—by the forlorn Roanoke Island colony, settled in 1585 under the leadership of Sir Walter Raleigh. An account written by one of the settlers reports: "Wee made of the same in the countrey some mault, whereof was brued as good ale as was to be desired."

During the early exploration of the American continent, beer was an essential beverage on ships. Plain water stagnated quickly on a long trip, while beer remained comparatively palatable. In addition, its dietetic makeup, though unidentified in those days, helped ward off many of the ills that seamen and passengers on long voyages were prone to.

History suggests that a shortage of beer on the *Mayflower* was partly responsible for the Pilgrims' unscheduled landing at Plymouth Rock. They had been heading south to Virginia when a shortage of provisions forced them to land at the tip of Cape Cod, at what is today Provincetown, Massachusetts, where they subsequently founded the Plymouth colony. In the Library of Congress a copy of the *Mayflower*'s logbook, dated December 19, 1620, bears this entry: "We could not now take time for further searche or consideration: our victuals being much spente, especially our beere."

Conceivably, had it not been for beer, some other rock or inlet on the Atlantic coast might now be famous as the place where the

William Penn's brewery in Pennsbury, Bucks County, Pennsylvania, circa 1690.

Pilgrims landed. According to the U.S. Brewers' Association, established in 1862, beer was the universal beverage of the Pilgrims. It was present at the first Thanksgiving along with turkey, lobster, oysters, venison, duck, and clams.

During the early colonization it is unlikely that there were more than a handful of commercial breweries, known then as "public" or "common" breweries. The first recorded commercial brewery in America was established in 1612 by a Dutchman and a Dane, Block and Christiansen, in New Amsterdam (New York). About a decade later the director-general of New Amsterdam, Peter Minuit, erected a municipal brewery, which continued until 1638, when it was forced to close by heavy competition from private brewers.

George Washington liked beer enough to have his own recipe. It is still preserved in his handwriting in the New York Public Library. During the Revolutionary War, General Washington heartily approved the soldiers' daily ration of a quart of beer, as established by the Continental Congress. William Penn, Samuel Adams, James Madison, and Patrick Henry were brewers. Thomas Jefferson, also a brewer, said of beer, "I wish to see this beverage become common." He went so far as to import European brewers to teach the art to Americans.

Despite involvement and encouragement by many American leaders, brewing could hardly have been called a strong industry in the early years before and after the American Revolution. Through the first few decades of the 19th century, brewing was practiced in a primitive way with simple equipment. Open-fire kettles in small sheds and underground or sidehill cellars or storage vaults comprised the common brewery. Natural ice was used for cooling when available, since there was no mechanical refrigeration. Much of the early beer was drunk warmer than modern tastes enjoy.

The first breweries were generally small operations, most of them producing only 150 to 200 barrels per year. It was a sizable business that brewed 300 to 400 barrels of beer annually. The breweries delivered their beer to taverns and residences, transporting the barrels in small carts or wheelbarrows. Customers often fetched beer themselves directly from the brewery in their own jugs or pails.

Toward the end of the 1840s, the brewing industry expanded out from the Eastern seaboard and moved westward with the rest

Brewing beer in an 1820 American brewery.

of the country. Cincinnati and Chicago became important brewing centers, then Detroit, Cleveland, St. Louis, and, of course, Milwaukee. By 1850 there were 431 commercial breweries, a figure that was to peak at 4,131 in 1873.

The Advent of Lager Beer

The great expansion of the brewing industry to the west was largely due to the tremendous popularity of a new type of beer introduced in the United States in the early 1840s. The extent to which beer is said to be our national drink attests to the importance of *lager* beer in this country.

Before 1840, all beers in America were of the ale, stout, and porter types—strong and malty, but flat British brews. *Lager,* the creation of unnamed German brewers, provided a hoppy, lighter-colored, milder-tasting, sparkling beer that immediately became more popular than the early brews. A different and highly coveted yeast was required for lager, and the beer fermented much longer in cool cellars (*lagern* means "to store"). During this period of rest its valuable properties of taste were developed. Lager beer revolutionized the American brewing industry by offering a lively foaming beer that was more palatable to most people than were the old-style beers.

The heightened popularity of beer, brought about by the introduction of lager, enabled the brewing industry to expand to the farthest reaches of the Western frontier. Wherever settlements blossomed in the West, the brewers were not far behind.

Chapter Two

Copper Kettles and Wooden Barrels

COMMERCIAL BREWING in the Pacific Northwest began in 1852, when a German immigrant named Henry Saxer established his Liberty Brewery at the new village called Portland in the Oregon Territory. He missed being the first brewer on the Pacific Coast by three years; that honor went to San Francisco brewer Adam Schuppert in 1849.

Saxer's modest beer plant, near what is now First and Davis Streets in downtown Portland, was the first of a number of early breweries in the salmon and timber country. In 1854 the second Northwest brewery was started by Nicholas Delin in Steilacoom. Walla Walla brewmaster Emil Meyer was next in 1855, followed in 1856 by John Muench of Fort Vancouver and J. J. Holman in Jacksonville. Martin Schmeig of Steilacoom opened a brewery in 1858, and in 1859 young Henry Weinhard bought the Muench brewery across the Columbia River from the city that would bring him fame.

Those seven were the vanguard in a growing parade of pioneer Northwest brewers who brought their art to a thirsty frontier. Introducing the careful brewing methods of the Old Country, these adventurous brewers set themselves the task of satisfying a limitless demand.

Although the major Eastern breweries did good business in the Northwest, many mining, logging, and farming towns had their own breweries soon after they were founded. Because road and rail systems were in their infancy, and beer kegs were heavy and bulky, distribution of the early beers was restricted to small geographical areas. As a result, new breweries sprang up like mushrooms during the 1860s and 1870s. A further factor in this growth was the advent of local hops and barley cultivation

Henry Saxer's Liberty Brewery, built in 1852, was the first commercial beer brewing plant in the Pacific Northwest.

around 1865. Before that, hops and malt had to be shipped to the Northwest from San Francisco. With the proliferation of breweries, peaking in the late 1870s, each city and town proudly boasted its own local beer.

Beer was sold in the saloons and also in "beer gardens," which sold nothing but beer. Despite the expression often heard in "B" westerns—"Whiskey, bartender, and leave the bottle"—in real life Westerners swallowed considerably more beer than the hard stuff.

Almost without exception the pioneer brewers were German. A few had non-German business partners over the years, but most of the brewers themselves were men who had apprenticed in the great brewing capitals of the German and Austrian Empires, such as Munich, Vienna, and Pilsen, then emigrated to America in search of better opportunities on this side of the Atlantic. Some of them learned their trade in the United States by working for established German brewers in the East.

The brewmasters who found their way to the Pacific Northwest were hardy entrepreneurs who became men of consequence and leadership in their communities. They arrived in Oregon and

Washington brewer John U. Hofstetter brought his six-barrel copper brewkettle 2,000 miles over the Oregon Trail.

Washington by different paths and at various stages in their lives. Henry Rust left his native Germany as a young brewer of twenty-three. Soon after arriving in America, he saw action in the Civil War, on the Union side, and was twice wounded. While in the service he saved his money, adding to it after the war by mining in Montana. In 1866 brewmaster Rust moved to Oregon and started a brewery in Clarksville, near the Burnt River placer diggings, and in 1874 built a brewery in Baker City.

In Colville, Washington, John U. Hofstetter started his brewery in 1861 with a six-barrel copper brewing kettle that he hauled 2,000 miles over the Oregon Trail. Another brewer, Jacob Betz, was apprenticed in a large German brewery at the age of fourteen. Arriving in America in 1860, he worked at breweries in New

York, Philadelphia, Cincinnati, and San Francisco before establishing his own brewery in Walla Walla in 1874. Though they came to the Pacific Northwest by different routes and means, all the brewers named in this book ultimately stayed to build 138 breweries in Washington and 126 in Oregon.

One common trait among the early brewers in the Northwest, as elsewhere, was their quest for excellence in the beer they made. Few callings have developed such zealous professional pride as the brewer has always possessed. His sole ambition was to produce a fine glass of beer. He was welcomed with his kettles and barrels wherever he chose to settle, for the Northwest miners, farmers, loggers, and fishermen had worked up a legendary thirst.

How the Brewer Made His Beer

Brewing is a simple yet fascinating process; except for modern refinements, it has hardly changed since the day in 1852 when Henry Saxer first offered a mug of cold beer to the town of Portland.

Successful beer-making begins with good water. The excellence, purity, and abundance of the water was significant in attracting brewers to the Pacific Northwest. Many of them set up

John Hofstetter's Colville brewery, circa 1880.

their businesses at the sites of natural artesian wells. Others merely had to drill a shallow well to tap the prolific water resources.

The first step in the manufacture of beer took place in the *malthouse,* where barley was soaked in water for about a day and a half. During this time the kernels absorbed a great deal of water and turned soft. The steeped barley was then transferred into large open bins, where it was allowed to germinate. That is, it came to life and began to sprout just as though it had been planted in warm, moist earth. When the rootlets were about twice the length of the kernel itself, the grain was again transferred into other large open bins in a warm room, where it was dried. This step was called *kilning* and took about twenty-four hours. The end product of this process was *barley malt,* the chief ingredient in the brewing of beer. The malting procedure was time-consuming and heavy work, since tons of grain were needed by the breweries. (Today only a handful of breweries in this country do their own malting. Most malt is purchased from malting firms.)

The next step in the brewing process was the grinding, or milling, of the malt grain in a brewery mill especially designed for that purpose. The ground malt was then mixed with pure water in a large wooden tub called a *mash tun.* In some breweries (almost all of them today), cooked corn or rice was added to the malt. The mixture was stirred by hand with long wooden paddles in the early smaller breweries, and by steam-powered machinery in larger operations. The result was called *malt mash* and had the consistency of cooked breakfast cereal.

The liquid portion of the mash was then strained off and channeled or piped into the large copper brewkettle. Here the liquid, called *wort* (pronouced "wert"), was boiled with hops, the dried cones of the hop vine that give beer its distinctive flavor and aroma. The boiling sterilized and concentrated the wort and released the flavor of the hops.

The copper brewkettles of the late 19th century were upright dome-shaped vessels having arched lids with an opening for the hops and a vent for the escape of steam. Almost every brewer had his own ideas and practices for cooking the wort and hops in the brewkettle.

After several hours of the boiling process, the flavored or hopped wort was transferred from the kettle through a strainer, or *hop-jack* (later called "hop-back"), which separated the hops from the wort. The strained, hopped wort was then run into shallow wort coolers, where it was quickly cooled. From there it was piped to a large vat called a *fermenting tun,* housed in a cool cellar or an ice chamber.

In the fermenting vat a special strain of brewer's yeast was added to the wort and allowed to ferment for a number of days. To make *lager* beer, a yeast that settled and fermented from the bottom was used. It worked slowly, taking from seven to eleven days for complete fermentation. Although lager was the popular brew in America, some Northwest breweries also made *ale,* and for that a top-fermenting yeast was used that was faster acting and fermented at a higher temperature.

After fermentation, most of the yeast was removed and the beer was decanted into wooden casks, where it remained for up to several months in the ice house for aging. As the beer aged, it clarified and the flavors became smooth and mellow.

Pails, Kegs, and Bottles

Beer produced in the early days was not readily available for consumption in the home. It was keg beer, intended for distribution through local taverns, dispensed from five-, ten-, and fifteen-gallon wooden kegs at 5¢ a glass. If father and mother wanted beer with supper, a child was sent scurrying to the neighborhood tavern, or to the brewery itself, for a pail of beer. Beer pails were common in kitchens before 1900, and heaven help anyone who inadvertently used the beer pail to store butter or beans. Two- and four-quart tin lard buckets were the usual vessels kept as beer pails. In addition, most breweries sold five-gallon wooden kegs for home use.

Bottled beer was not unknown in this country in the 1860s and 1870s, but for many years the brewers were averse to bottling their beers. In the first place, it was easier and cheaper to distribute beer in bulk kegs through established outlets. Also, a peculiar quirk in the federal tax laws during the early years stipulated that beer be transported across a public highway to a separate plant for bottling. This was a costly operation for the small Northwest breweries. Finally, it was found that no matter how well the beer was brewed, it often turned sour in the bottle.

By the mid-1880s the public's demand for bottled beer, together with new processes to prevent spoilage, motivated many

In the 19th century beer was commonly carried from tavern to home in one-gallon tin lard pails. This one was used by a Spokane family in the 1890s.

Oregon and Washington breweries to offer their products in bottles as well as the time-honored kegs. Some were slow to "go modern," and did not bottle their beer until much later. The Roseburg (Oregon) *Plaindealer* reported on November 28, 1901: "Max Weiss, the brewer, has added a bottling machine to his brewery plant with a capacity of 200 bottles per hour, which is a valuable improvement."

The average beer bottle in the 1880s was made of green glass, held a quart of beer, and had a cork. (Brown glass did not become popular until after Prohibition.) Some breweries embossed their names in the glass, and others began using paper labels.

Plain corks began to be replaced as stoppers on beer bottles in the Northwest by the early 1880s, when a number of other types of closures were invented. In 1892 the "crown cork closure" came into use, with a thin slice of cork inside a tight-fitting metal cap. A similar type of cap (with plastic instead of cork) is common to this day on most beer bottles.

Cans came into use as beer containers in 1935. The first can style was the "cone top," named for its shape, which could be

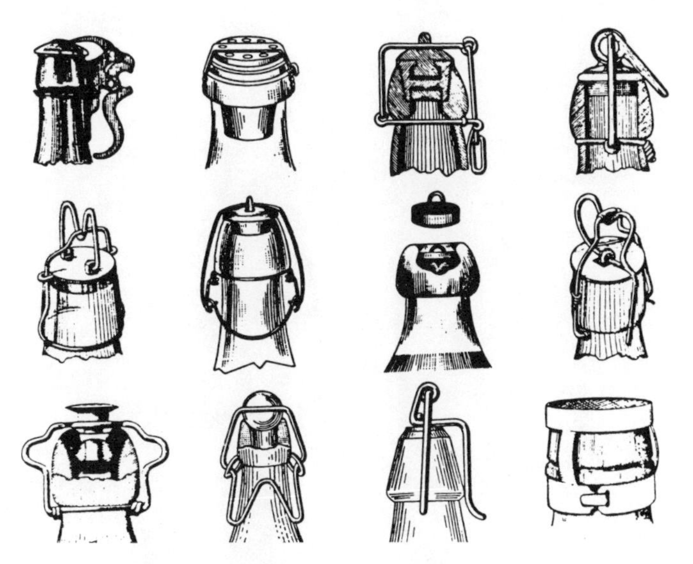

A few examples of the 333 types of beer bottle stoppers patented in the United States between 1880 and 1890.

filled by bottling equipment already in place with only minor adjustment of the machinery. Next came the "flat top" style—for which an opener, colloquially known as a "church key," was required—then the "pull tab," and, finally, the present "punch tab."

The Never-Ending Need for Ice, Ice, Ice!

The early breweries required huge amounts of block ice all year round to process and store their beverages. Before the invention of artificial ice-making machines, brewers depended on the availability of natural ice to supply their ice houses. In most parts of the Northwest, natural ice could be cut from frozen winter lakes. Breweries west of the Cascades, where moderate winter temperatures seldom allowed ice to form on local lakes, had to get it from high in the mountains. Breweries located in central and eastern Washington and Oregon, where the winters were colder, could harvest their ice from lakes and ponds at lower elevations.

But in some areas, such as along the coast, finding suitable ice was a constant problem. In fact, the situation was so critical to early coastal brewers that the Alaska Ice Company was formed in Sitka, Alaska to cut, store, and ship block ice to the west coast of

Harvesting brewery ice in 1890 from an eastern Washington lake.

the United States, where they sold their precious cargo at a high price.

The procedure for obtaining natural ice was expensive and time-consuming. In the winter, crews and horses were hired to find, cut, and transport the ice to the breweries—often at long distances. Seasoned ice crews would scout for lakes where the ice was at least ten inches thick. Initial cuts in the ice were made by V-shaped horse-drawn plows. Then horse-powered saws were used to saw the ice to a depth of about six inches. The next step was the back-breaking labor of hand-sawing the ice into cakes about two feet square. The heavy cakes were then hoisted by pulley into a wagon or sled for the trip to the brewery.

At the brewery, the blocks of ice were lifted by horse-drawn or steam-powered pulley into a chute and pulled up into the ice

Poling ice rafts to shore.

The coming of ice-making machines was a real boon to breweries. This massive unit, made by the Harris Ice Machine Works in Portland, could manufacture 125 tons of block ice every twenty-four hours. (Photo from the 1903 Harris catalog.)

house, where they were packed in sawdust or straw for storage through the warm summer months. Some breweries kept their ice underground in cellars.

The advent of ice-making machines in the 1880s was heralded by brewers across the country, including the Northwest, as an important advance in their craft. No longer were they dependent on the vagaries of weather for production of the tons of ice needed by their breweries.

On the consumers' end, too, ice was essential to the beer industry. Americans, unlike most Europeans, preferred their beer served cold. With the coming of mechanical ice-making processes, the breweries had an unending supply of pure, fresh ice and could deliver it generously to the taverns that carried their beers.

The basic design of the early ice machines was based on the principle of heat absorption. Certain gases such as ammonia and ether absorbed heat when liquefied under pressure, thus producing cold when allowed to expand. These cold-producing compression devices were constructed to apply the cold to water and make ice. Such revolutionary ice-making machines as the York,

The *Mt. Hood* ice machine was the smallest model made by the Harris Ice Machine Works. It could crank out one ton of ice per day and was popular with some of the low-capacity local breweries in the Northwest.

NORTH PACIFIC BREWERY.

JOHN KOPP, PROPRIETOR.

ASTORIA, *OREGON.*

Patronize Home Industry.

WE SUPPLY AS GOOD A QUALITY OF

As any in the Market

at as

Reasonable a Price.

Pure and Unadulterated Gives General Satisfaction, and is Furnished in Any Quantity.

DAILY DELIVERY IN THE CITY. P. O. BOX 40.

WE ALSO HAVE CONNECTED WITH THE BREWERY

An Extensive Ice Plant

Where a Superior Quality of Pure Crystal Ice is Manufactured and supplied to the consumers in quantities to suit.

An abundant supply of clean ice was essential for brewing and consumer needs, as shown in this 1898 advertisement for John Kopp's North Pacific Brewery in Astoria.

Eclipse, and Triumph, all made in the East, found their way to Northwest breweries. Later, some of the most popular ice-making machines were manufactured in the Northwest by the Harris Ice Machine Works in Portland, and by the Armstrong Machine Company of Spokane.

The production and selling of ice became an adjunct to the brewing industry, and many local breweries provided a regular ice service to hotels, restaurants, and private homes. Some breweries even offered cold-storage services for the preservation of perishable goods.

Tall Windows and Stately Walls: Brewery Architecture

The construction of the 19th-century breweries required careful and innovative planning to accommodate the various brewing processes. Competent engineering skills and sturdy construction were needed for the huge vats holding large amounts of liquid, the heavy bins of grain, and the rooms containing tons of ice. The beer storage rooms were cooled by mountains of ice kept in chambers above. Imagine ice chambers twenty feet deep, filled to the top with blocks of ice having a combined weight of 1,150 pounds per square foot.

Equipment was arranged for efficiency and to take advantage of gravity wherever possible. Grain storage and milling was often located high in the brewery on the third or fourth floor or in a rooftop structure. During mashing, the milled grist (malt) dropped into the mash tun below. The copper brewkettle was commonly located beneath the mash tun at ground level. The large vat and tanks were made of oak, redwood, or cedar and had hand-hewn staves that were often sixteen feet high.

This multi-level arrangement of equipment and machinery resulted in architecture that was quite beautiful, with the lofty brewhouse tower looming high in the air, often decorated with castle-like turrets and parapets, and capped by a flagpole with the Stars and Stripes flying at the top. Tall windows to let in light and air broke the stately brick walls.

Some of the larger brewing plants in the Northwest were little cities in themselves, with their brewhouse, malthouse, bottling works (across the road by federal law), barns and stables, powerhouse, palatial offices, warehouses, and homes for the brewmaster and his assistants. The brewery came to be more than a workshop, more than a factory, more than an office—in many cases it became an outstanding ornament of the community and a showplace for the visitor.

Not all Northwest breweries were large and showy; many were modest structures. But even in the smaller towns of Oregon and Washington, the local brewery, usually a handsome brick building with white stone or painted wood trim, was one of the most impressive buildings in the community.

As a group, the brewers themselves were a happy, generous lot, quick to help out with free kegs of beer at community picnics,

Fourth of July celebrations, and fundraising events. They were respected citizens, proud of their calling and of their contribution to the settlement and industry of the Pacific Northwest.

In this 1900 photograph, brewmaster Max Weiss stands beside a beer wagon at his Roseburg Brewing & Ice Company in Roseburg, Oregon, while employees display bottles of their frothy product.

Chapter Three

Brewed in Oregon

OREGON HAS HAD 126 licensed breweries from 1852 to the present. Much is known about some of them, including anecdotes handed down through descendants of the old-time brewers and stories reported in the newspapers of the day. But time has dropped a veil over others, leaving us with scanty information. In some cases only the brewers' names and approximate dates of operation remain.

In memory of those early Northwesterners, whose primary goal in life was to brew a good glass of beer, here are the breweries of Oregon.

ALBANY

Albany had three breweries. The first was simply called the Albany Brewery. It was established in 1873 at the southwest corner of Broadalbin and Water Streets by Charles Kiefer and a partner named Rogers. Kiefer brewed a popular local beer for twelve years, though his output was not large; in 1878, for example, he sold only 180 barrels. In that same year brewmaster Kiefer took on a new business partner, John B. Natter, and in 1886 they sold the brewery to Adam Luchsinger, who ran it for two years. In 1888 George Pfau purchased the plant, changed the name to Star Brewery, and continued operating for four years until closing the doors for good in 1891.

The second brewery was established in 1874 as the Bellanger Brewery by Edward I. Bellanger. It was located on the southwest corner of First and Baker Streets. His modest brewery was in business for ten years. In 1879 he produced 345 barrels of lager.

The third brewery was by far the largest and was no doubt a factor in the ultimate demise of the other two. In 1884 William

At the turn of the century the Albany Brewing and Bottling Company in Albany, Oregon was producing 8,000 barrels of beer annually. The large size of the plant cannot be seen from this rare print.

and Paul Faber began what was to become the largest brewery in the Willamette Valley, the Albany Brewing and Bottling Company. The grand complex on the northeast corner of Ninth and Lyon was for many years an Albany landmark.

The brewery manufactured 8,000 barrels of beer yearly and employed a force of twenty men. The company had a standing order with an outlet in San Francisco for 25 barrels of beer each week. The 1902 Albany City Directory lauded the Fabers' enterprise: "The product of this plant is acknowledged to have excellent tonic and strengthening properties and [is] a beverage that gives health to all who drink it, especially the nursing mother and convalescent." The brewery also had an ice plant that turned out six tons of ice daily.

William Faber sold his brewery in 1906 to the burgeoning Salem Brewery Association for use as their Albany branch plant. After two years under SBA ownership, the brewery was closed in 1908.

ASHLAND

In 1884 Charles Wurz operated a short-term brewery, and a competitor advertised in the May 29, 1885 *Rogue River Courier*:

ASHLAND BREWERY
Reitel & Co., Prop.
Kegs and Bottle Beer

Neither of these breweries lasted more than a couple of years. Ashland was primarily supplied with beer from the two established breweries in nearby Jacksonville, and at the turn of the century by breweries in Medford, Roseburg, and Portland.

ASTORIA

The first brewer to ply his trade in this seafarer's town at the mouth of the Columbia River was Michael Myers, who built a brewery in 1872. Before that, Astorians quenched their thirst with beer brought downriver from Portland. The Myers brewery stayed in business for twelve years. In 1878, he sold 866 barrels of beer.

Myers' chief competitor was fellow German brewer John Hahn, who with his partner E. Papmahl established a brewery on Concomly (now Astor) Street in 1874. The Hahn-Papmahl brewery operated for ten years. It was sold in 1884 to the St. Louis Brewing Company. They ran it for another eleven years under the St. Louis label, but closed the brewery in 1895. As for John Hahn, the likable brewmaster gave up his life of hops and wort to become Astoria's leading boot and shoe dealer.

For a short time Astoria had the distinction of having a woman brewer. Theresa O'Brien ran a small ale brewery from 1886 through 1887.

The largest brewery in town was John Kopp's North Pacific Brewery, established in 1884. Kopp, who immigrated to the United States at twenty years of age, first started the Bay View Brewery in Seattle in 1883, then moved south to Astoria the next year to found the North Pacific Brewery. At its peak, production was 15,000 barrels of beer per year. Kopp also manufactured 90 tons of ice each month. He employed from ten to fifteen brewery workers and supplied not only the city of Astoria, but all coastal points south to Tillamook.

John Kopp's North Pacific Brewery was Astoria's largest beer maker. At the time of this photo in 1910, the waterfront brewery produced 15,000 barrels of beer yearly. Notice the beer wagon loaded with barrels ready for distribution.

A devastating fire in the summer of 1889 leveled the North Pacific Brewery. John Kopp rebuilt on the same site, enlarging both the brewery and ice house. His business flourished, and in 1905 he opened a branch brewery in Portland at 18th and Upshur, with a downtown sales office.

John Kopp's imposing Astoria brewery, at 31st Street and Franklin Avenue, continued in business until 1916. The old North Pacific Brewery beer storage building was remodeled as a fire station in 1928 and stands today, at 2968 Marine Drive, as a fire department museum.

BAKER

An enterprising, friendly young brewer from Bavaria, Louis Kastner, saw an opportunity in the growing community of Baker City, the financial and trade center for a vast mining area. Kastner had been working for two years in F. C. Sels's brewery in Canyon City, to the southwest, and thought it was time to go into business for himself. With a partner named Joseph Lachner, Louis established the Kastner & Lachner Brewery in 1872.

Louis had an outgoing, happy, generous disposition, and was popular among the citizens of Baker County. And he enjoyed the advantage of having the only brewery in the district. But he was not without competition for long. In 1874 Henry Rust, a former Clarksville brewer, came back to Oregon and saw a market for *two* beer makers in Baker City (a view not likely shared by Louis Kastner) and promptly built his own plant, the Pacific Brewery.

The competition between the two brewers was legendary. Each tried to outdo the other in community goodwill and marketing. If Louis Kastner promised four barrels of his fine lager for the July 4th town picnic, Henry Rust promised five. Once, in 1879, Herr Kastner won hearts and applause by sponsoring an engagement of a touring dance troupe from New York. In response, Henry Rust immediately set about building an opera hall, which hosted a wide variety of entertainers until well into this century.

In 1880 Louis Kastner changed the name of his business to the City Brewery, and the competition with his rival continued. For example, in the February 22, 1882 issue of the Baker City *Bedrock Democrat*, Kastner placed a sedate little 2″ × 2″ ad proclaiming: "City Brewery—Louis Kastner—bottled and keg lager beer." On the next page was a 7″ × 7″ ad for the "Pacific Brewery, Henry Rust, Proprietor." And so it went.

In the end, Henry Rust outlasted his friend. In 1885 Louis Kastner sold his brewery to Julius Lachs and William Widman, said goodbye to Henry, and moved to San Diego as agent for the U.S. Brewing Company of Portland.

Lachs and Widman operated the City Brewery for two years, then went out of business.

The year 1885 was a good one for Henry Rust; his old friendly rival Kastner was gone, and the new owners of City Brewery were not as competitive. Baker City was an excellent market for beer, and Henry took advantage of it by expanding the site of his brewery. In that year there were fourteen saloons in town, serving an area population of close to 8,000, including miners, ranchers, cowboys, and sheepherders. The Pacific Brewery now had a capacity of 10,000 barrels of lager per year.

Pioneer brewer Henry Rust established his Pacific Brewery and an opera house in the gold rush town of Baker in northeastern Oregon.

Henry Rust worked at his trade until 1903. When he was nearing seventy, he sold his beloved Pacific Brewery at Third and Dewey to Reinhard Martin of Spokane, who renamed it the American Brewing and Crystal Ice Company. And so it remained until state prohibition closed its doors in 1916.

A man named Carl Stofft also ran a small brewing operation in Baker City from 1904 until 1916, but little is known about it.

A further note on Louis Kastner: Louis quickly tired of California and moved back to Baker City, but this time he did not try to open his own brewery. Instead, he went to work as a master brewer for his former friendly nemesis, Henry Rust. Louis was as cheerful and popular as ever, but without his past business worries. He had an acclaimed singing voice and was a member of his church choir. The *Bedrock Democrat* said of him, "His powers as a vocalist render him popular in social circles where music is always a feature of entertainment." And assuredly, his powers as a *Bräumeister* rendered him equally popular.

BANDON

Longtime Oregon brewer John Gottlieb Mehl had the misfortune to die just as he was establishing the first brewery in the coastal community of Bandon in 1892. (See Mr. Mehl's story in the Coquille and Roseburg sections.) His wife, Mary, finished the brewery on Iris Street and ran it for three years. In 1896 she sold it to Joseph Walser, a brewer from nearby Randolph. Walser sold the Bandon Brewery in 1904 to George C. Gehrig, who made lager there until 1910.

BROWNSVILLE

Mr. B. Clomer held a brewery license in this Linn County town in 1878 and 1879, but there is no record that a brewery was built or that any beer was actually made. Perhaps he couldn't brew up enough support or financing to get going.

BURNS

The first brewery to supply a refreshing local lager in this Harney County desert community was the Locher Brewery, established on Third Street in 1888. Paul Locher, a German immigrant *Bräumeister,* arrived in Harney County in 1887 and built his brewery just four years after the town was founded. He stayed to brew beer for almost twenty years, becoming one of Burns' leading business figures. John Rohrman and Michael Pankvatz were two of his brewery partners over the years.

The May 2, 1902 edition of the *Harney County News* carried this ad:

THE LOCHER BREWERY BEER
Furnishes a first-class malt beverage.
Actual test shows it to be of greater
specific strength than imported beer.
It is a home product, and suits.
Order a trial keg and be convinced of
its excellence.
LOCHER BREWERY BURNS, OREGON

Locher built a home and social hall, Locher's Hall, which was used for weddings, graduations, dances, and receptions because it was the only large facility in town. He also owned a number of other properties, including innovative underground warehouses. Paul Locher ran his brewery until 1905.

The second brewery in Burns was built in 1898 by Louis Woldenberg and a partner named Berg on what became known as "Brewery Hill." They called their new plant the Harney Valley Brewery.

Competing with Paul Locher's brewery, Woldenberg and Berg placed this ad in the June 8, 1901 *Times-Herald*:

HARNEY VALLEY BREWERY
Quart bottles delivered in Burns
$1.50 per dozen
5-gal. kegs $2.00 delivered
to your home in Burns.
telephone no. 5
Woldenberg & Berg

The prices alone are enough to quicken the pulse of modern beer-lovers.

In 1905 Louis Woldenberg sold his brewery to John and Tom Jenkins. The Jenkins brothers replaced the wooden structure with a massive stone building and called it the Harney Valley Brewing Company. They operated the brewery for seven years, closing it in 1912.

The stone brewery building is gone, and the site at Broadway and D Street is now occupied by the Harney County Museum and the Burns Chamber of Commerce.

CANYON CITY

John H. Stahl was born in Germany in 1825. He apprenticed in the brewing trade at thirteen, and later attended Europe's pre-eminent brewing school at Worms. When John was twenty-five he immigrated to America, came west to San Francisco, and worked for some years as a brewer. In 1862 Stahl and his wife moved north to booming Canyon City in eastern Oregon.

The word in Canyon City was "gold." An estimated $26 million in gold was mined in the district. Thousands of miners flocked to the area: 5,000 to Canyon Creek gulch, and another 5,000 to the valley above. They were quickly followed by tradesmen, saloon-keepers, gamblers, and "ladies of ultimate accessibility." By late fall 1862, there were twelve saloons in the new settlement.

Bräumeister F. C. Sels, owner of the City Brewery of Canyon City, Oregon, came to America from Germany. He was also a county judge.

In this gold rush turmoil John Stahl built a brewery and was immediately successful. He looked after his Canyon City Brewery and also held an active interest in the rich Prairie Diggings Mine until 1870. In that year Stahl sold the brewery to his friend F. C. Sels and moved to Walla Walla, where he continued in the brewing profession for many years. (See Walla Walla, Washington section.)

Francis C. Sels, like Stahl, came to America from Germany as a young man, and kept going west to California. He joined the rush to eastern Oregon gold and was one of the first businessmen in Canyon City, opening a general store there in the spring of 1863. He was a justice of the peace from 1864 until 1866; in 1870 he was elected county judge. In that year, too, he became owner of the Canyon City Brewery.

It's good that Judge Sels was of sturdy, stable pioneer stock, because just two weeks after he purchased the brewery it was destroyed by one of three devastating fires that swept through Canyon City over the years. He rebuilt it at once with large fire-proof stone blocks, and the brewery was soon back in business, with the addition of an attached saloon. He renamed it the City Brewery.

With various assistant brewers and business partners, such as Louis Kastner, John Kuhl, and Henry Breyer, F. C. Sels brewed lager in Canyon City for the next 42 years.

The historic Sels brewery still stands, restored by Canyon City's "Whiskey Gulch Gang" in 1972. The large stone building, with its swinging doors and sawdust floors, is a favorite center for special events during the annual " '62 Days" celebration.

After a disastrous Canyon City fire burned the F. C. Sels brewery to the ground in 1870, he rebuilt with large fireproof stones and continued brewing beer for the next 42 years. F. C. Sels, with his long white beard, is seated next to the little boy.

CANYONVILLE

Leonard Stenger, a brewer from Bavaria, was one of the earliest pioneer settlers in this historic Douglas County community. He farmed on his Donation Land Claim property from 1854 until 1874. With new growth and settlement in the area, he decided to revert to his Old Country training and open a brewery.

Early Douglas County newspapers reported a controversy that began when he built his brewery directly across the road from the first Canyonville school, but except for small boys trying to sneak in to sample his product from time to time, his location caused no real problems.

The Stenger Brewery was in business for ten years, from 1874 to 1884.

CLARKSVILLE

The first brewery in Baker County was operated by Henry Rust in 1866 in the settlement of Clarksville, near the Burnt River placer diggings. He had run the brewery for about two years when he decided to move to South America. He sold the brewery to August Frunk, who ran it until 1874.

COALEDO

This short-lived coal mining community in the Coos Bay area had a small brewery from 1874 to 1875 that was run by Henry Tolle.

COOS BAY

The first brewery in Coos County was in Marshfield, renamed Coos Bay in 1944. It was built in 1868 by George Stauf and William Reichert, but it had a succession of owners through its 44-year history.

In 1874 Stauf sold his interest to Reichert and started another brewery in nearby Utter City. William Reichert continued brewing Marshfield's beer until 1882, when he sold to Lars Clemmensen and a man named Evanoff. They operated the brewery until 1901.

An Englishman, Robert Marsden, was the next owner. He purchased the plant in 1901, called it the Marshfield Brewing Company, and hired an experienced brewmaster, Herman Roswinkle, to manage the business. Marsden himself was not a brewer by trade; he was the owner of several businesses in the area, including the Riverton Coal Company. He also owned a tavern in town, and he opened another saloon that was attached to the brewery itself, a common practice in those days, calling it the Brewery Saloon.

Robert Marsden continued in the brewery business for six years, until 1907, when another reorganization resulted in new owners and a corporate name change to Coos Bay Eagle Brewing Company, while the plant itself was called the Bayview Brewery. The brewery finally closed in 1912.

There were two other short-term breweries in Marshfield. One was owned by Robert Peters and a partner named Kling in 1904, and the other was run by Schaufel and Youngmayr in 1910.

Also, in 1904 the Coos Bay Bottling Works on Front Street advertised the bottling of Portland's Gambrinus Beer in quarts, pints, and half-pints, "Family Orders Welcomed."

COQUILLE

John Gottlieb Mehl brewed lager beer at his City Brewery in Coquille City for eighteen years, from 1874 through 1892. This little, likable, generous immigrant, born in Württemberg in southwest Germany in 1823, was a true Oregon pioneer. He arrived in Philadelphia in 1844, and five years later he came across the plains to what is now Roseburg in Douglas County. There he was granted a Donation Land Claim (land given to pioneers who came into the Oregon Territory before 1855). In 1861 he founded a brewery in Roseburg, taking John Rast as a partner in 1866. After a fire burned the business in 1871 Mehl moved to Oakland, Oregon, where he opened a brewery, and he settled at Coquille in 1877.

The delicious lager brewed by *Bräumeister* Mehl was widely acclaimed in the region. He sold only keg beer, and his five-gallon "home kegs" were especially popular with the rural people in the district who didn't get into town often. His ten- and fifteen-gallon kegs went to taverns, restaurants, and logging camps, and of course much of the beer was sold right at the brewery.

A devastating 1889 fire destroyed the Mehl brewery, but the brewer rebuilt with the help of the community. After that he made a habit of giving free beer to all the men on the fire brigade when they came back from fighting a fire.

In 1892 Gottlieb Mehl decided to open an additional brewery in nearby Bandon. He had almost completed construction of the new plant when he died on April 24, 1893. The longtime Coquille Brewery was closed by Gottlieb's widow Mary, and she controlled the Bandon plant for three years.

CORVALLIS

There were two breweries in Corvallis. The first one was built in 1872 by Bernard Hunt. He sold in 1875 to Henry Hughes, who kept the brewery until 1879. It was a modest operation; Henry's brew production in 1878 amounted to 183 barrels, primarily sold by keg to local saloons.

Ignatz Furst bought the brewery in 1879, and he sold it in 1880 to John Zeis. Zeis called it the U.S. Brewery and was in business for ten years, finally closing the doors for good in 1890.

The other brewery in town was started in the spring of 1882 by John Riley and a man named Fischer. It was located on First Street, on the west bank of the Willamette River. Riley's Corvallis Brewery had an annual production rate of 1,500 barrels. It also closed in 1890.

COTTONWOOD

Cottonwood was a tiny settlement near Lakeview in Lake County. In 1884 Anton Melzer had a license to operate a brewery, but there is no record of production.

ENTERPRISE

The brewery in this Wallowa County community was built by the Ott brothers, Fritz and Frank, in 1898. They called it the Enterprise Brewing Company, and they made beer there through 1906. There was a saloon attached.

EUGENE

There were two breweries in Eugene. The oldest and largest was built in 1866 at Ninth and Olive by L. Burns. Little is recorded about Burns, but it is known that he ran his Eugene City Brewery for seven years, then sold it to August Werner and Henry Hagerman in 1873. Werner and Hagerman kept the immense, barn-like three-story brewery about a year before they disposed of it to Mathias Miller.

The Eugene City Brewery (later the Union Cold Storage, Ice & Brewing Co.) is shown here with its twin smokestacks. The brewery was located at Ninth Avenue (now Broadway) and Olive Street.

Under Mr. Miller's ownership the brewery had a capacity of 500 barrels per year, although in 1878 his production was only 114 barrels.

In 1881 Miller sold the brewery to Michael and Joseph Vogl. The Vogls changed the name to the Union Cold Storage, Ice & Brewing Co. and operated it for nine years.

The final owner of the original L. Burns brewery was Henry Weinhard, the Portland brew king, who purchased it in 1890. Not long after he bought the Ninth Avenue brewery, Henry shut down its beer-making operation. Thereafter the big barn with the twin smokestacks was known as Weinhard's Beer and Ice Depot. Only the ice was produced locally. Henry's beer, in bottles and kegs, was shipped from his Portland brewery. In 1914 the old brewery building was sold and torn down.

The other brewery in Eugene was owned by Eugene Weidmann from 1886 to 1891. It was a modest enterprise about which little is known. It was located on the northeast corner of Seventh Avenue and Olive Street.

MANUFACTURERS of WAGONS & BUGGIES

Wagons repaired in the best manner, and also made to order. Our facilities for the manufacture of wagons cannot be excelled and we would invite farmers to call at our establishment.

BREWERY.

AUGUST WERNER, Eugene City,

Dealer in and

MANUFACTURER OF BEER,

Which is sold by the barrel, half barrel or bottle. Families in the city supplied with Beer at their houses free of expressage.

All orders in city or country receive prompt attention.

J. J. COMSTOCK, Proprietor.

This is the most commodious Livery Stable in the Willamette Valley.

Advertisement for August Werner's brewery in Eugene, from an 1873 business directory. Brewmaster Werner promised free home delivery.

GARDINER

B. M. Akerblad established a small brewery in this coastal community in 1874. The brewery was purchased in 1878 by Frank Varrelmann and his partner Brant. They ran the brewery and a saloon until 1905. The old Varrelmann brewery still stands at Front and Spring Streets, and is now an apartment building.

GERVAIS

This small Marion County community had a brewery, owned by Glaser and Kirk, from 1879 to 1890. In 1879 they sold 129 barrels of beer.

GRANTS PASS

William Neurath established the Grants Pass Brewery in January 1887 at the site of his 30-foot artesian well, where Gilbert Creek crossed Front (now G) Street. He hired a brewer from Portland to take charge, and they built a reputation for fine lager. In 1891 he sold the brewery to Eugene Kienlen. A fire destroyed the plant in 1902, but by year's end he was back in business in a new brick building, with attached saloon, at the same site. Kienlen died in 1904 and his wife Marie continued the operation until Josephine County voted to "go dry" in 1908.

The Grants Pass Brewery building was renovated in 1975 and is now a fine restaurant at 509 Southwest G Street. The owners have carefully preserved the flavor of the historic brewery with old photographs, glass cases filled with antique beer bottles, old beer signs, and wooden barrels.

A second brewery, also on Gilbert Creek in Grants Pass, was started by a German immigrant named George Walter in 1891. He brewed beer for bottles and kegs at his Rogue River Brewery until 1897. According to an 1893 history, "He has a wagon delivery and does a large retail business. The brewery has a manufacturing capacity of five barrels daily, and the product of this brewery is considered to be very fine."

There was the beginning of a third brewery in 1905, but it did not have a chance to get going and closed at the end of the year. It was called the Eagle Brewing Company, and was located on the south side of the Rogue River.

The Grants Pass Brewery produced beer from 1887 until 1908. In 1975 the building was made into a restaurant. "The Brewery" dining house still retains the atmosphere and many artifacts of the old brewery.

HEPPNER

A. J. Stevenson started the first brewery in this Morrow County community in 1880. He sold it the next year to a German brewer named William Roesch. Brewmaster Roesch also kept this brewery for one year, selling it in 1882 to move to Pendleton, where he was a well-known brewer for many years.

The next owner of the City Brewery at Heppner was John B. Natter. Herr Natter was an experienced brewmaster who immigrated to America in 1854 and worked his trade in Illinois, Idaho, and California before coming to Oregon in 1868. He worked for a year at a Portland brewery, then went to Albany, where he was a partner in the Albany Brewery. Next he owned a Pendleton brewery, and at the same time, in 1882, Natter bought the Heppner City Brewery. According to an ad running in the Heppner *Gazette* from 1883 to 1890, Natter's City Brewery made more than just lager:

CITY BREWERY
Main Street, Heppner
Lager, Ale & Porter
Bottled Beer
Please return empty kegs

John Natter continued the brewery until his retirement in 1902.

ISLAND CITY

The Ott brothers, Fritz and Frank, had a small brewery in Island City, near La Grande, from 1889 to 1892. Later they owned the brewery in Enterprise.

JACKSONVILLE

The first of two breweries in this historic southern Oregon gold-mining town was established in 1856 by J. J. Holman in a small wood-frame house on Oregon Street. Little is known about the early years of the Eagle Brewery or of Mr. Holman, but it is known that J. J. sold the brewery in 1859 to Joseph Wetterer, about whom the records tell more.

Joseph Wetterer was a brewer in Baden in southwest Germany before crossing the Atlantic to America in 1850. He mined in

California, then moved north in 1853 to the new boom town of Jacksonville. He accumulated a stake in the first few years in Oregon and acquired the brewery.

Wetterer soon set about rebuilding the plant, adding a separate saloon and a residence on the property. By 1860 he was at full production as southern Oregon's only commercial brewery. Later his friend Veit Schutz opened the City Brewery and began a decades-long friendly rivalry for the area beer trade.

The Eagle's *Bräumeister* Wetterer believed in advertising, as did most of the brewers, and he kept a steady run of colorful ads and publicity items in the newspapers. In the October 10, 1863 *Oregon Sentinel*, Joseph proclaimed: "If you want a glass or keg of lager to drive away the blues, go to Wetterer's Brewery. His brew cannot be beat."

Joseph Wetterer died at the age of 50 in 1879, leaving a wife, Fredericka, and seven daughters. The widow Wetterer continued operating the brewery with help from loyal, experienced employees, particularly William Heeley, whom she married on June 5, 1883.

This small building at 355 South Oregon Street housed the Eagle Brewery Saloon. The brewery was in the rear. Now an artist's studio, it is the last remaining structure from Jacksonville's oldest brewery.

Though his expression is formal in this photograph, Veit Schutz was known in Jacksonville as the cheerful, generous proprietor of the City Brewery.

Even the gracious Sisters at St. Mary's Academy helped out, by bartering for young Josephine and Daisy Wetterer's usual $10 per term tuition in exchange for beer. Evidently the Sisters also enjoyed a cool sip from time to time.

William and Fredericka Heeley ran the brewery until 1890, then closed the doors for the last time.

The building that housed the Eagle Brewery Saloon, built in 1861 by Joseph Wetterer, still stands. It is now a private residence and art studio at 355 South Oregon Street. The brewery buildings, long gone, stood about 60 feet behind the saloon.

Veit Schutz was the other brewer in Jacksonville. He built his City Brewery in 1861 at the west end of California Street on the side of a small knoll. It was a good location, adjacent to the Jackson Creek mining operations on the west and the main population center of Jacksonville on the east.

Veit Schutz was born in Bavaria in 1823, where he was in the brewing business from the age of thirteen. His generosity and friendliness quickly made him one of Jacksonville's favorite adopted sons. The saloon attached to his brewery was a popular gathering place for Jacksonville businessmen and miners. Veit also constructed a large ballroom in an upper floor of the brewery, where many dances, weddings, performances, and receptions were held. One Jacksonville old-timer recalled that even roller skating and gymnastics were done at Schutz Hall.

But in 1864, even with the early success and popularity that Veit enjoyed, he was not a truly happy man. He was 41 and still single, a condition the cheerful brewer wanted strongly to change. So on March 12, 1864, he placed the following announcement in Jacksonville's *Oregon Intelligencer*: "Veit Schutz requests us to say to the marriageable ladies that he is on the marry; that he is not old, nor young, nor is he extremely ugly, or handsome; he is not rich, nor is he poor, but makes good lager, and has a comfortable and well-furnished house; that as he is desirous of marrying, he will not be very particular, so if the lady is not very old or very young, moderate size; if not handsome, not to be considered ugly; to be a good housekeeper, and not too extravagant; not to be a scold, but have fair spunk; if not rich, to have a fair portion of the spondulix. Yet the last item will be easily dispensed if the previous ones exist. If this should have the desired effect, he promises to advertise in the *Intelligencer*."

Veit did ultimately marry—twice. He married Josephine Rollmann in 1866, but unfortunately lost her. In 1883 he married Johanna Libge. Brewmaster Schutz and his wives had four children, the last one, son Gustof, born when he was 63 years old.

Veit Schutz died in 1892. Frank Theising acquired the City Brewery, but closed it in 1894. The brewery buildings were used for storage for some years, then stood empty for half a century, peopled only by ghosts of a former time. The vintage shell was finally torn down in 1976.

Evidence of the stone cellar of the City Brewery can be seen near the north entrance to the Britt Gardens on California Street.

JOSEPH

There were two breweries in Joseph. The first was built in 1889 by G. W. Hulery and a partner named Binswange, and operated for two years.

John Rohrman had the other brewery. Located on Main Street, it was in business from 1902 until 1906. Rohrman was from Burns and Sumpter, where he had been in the brewing business.

Rohrman's "Joseph Beer" was popular just after the turn of the century and was widely advertised by area saloons. The large brick brewery building still stands and has been converted to private living quarters.

JUNCTION CITY

The Junction City Brewery was in business from 1878 until 1888, under several different owners. Braun and Seeger built the modest brewery but only had it for a year. Then came H. R. Linke, who owned it from 1879 to 1882. Adolph Jaissle was the next owner, for two years, and the brewery was finally acquired by Eugene Weidmann, a brewer from nearby Eugene. The records

The financially plagued Junction City Brewery, shown here in 1887, had five owners in its short life.

show that Weidmann closed the Junction City Brewery in 1888, the same year he bought it. Presumably he then marketed lager beer in Junction City from his Eugene plant.

KLAMATH FALLS

John A. Uerlings came to America from Germany in 1847. Lured by California gold, he crossed the plains in '58, settling in Yreka. He worked as a brewer for twenty years in northern California, then moved to Linkville (Klamath Falls) in Oregon. There he purchased four lots on the corner of First and Main, where he built a brewery and a home. John Uerlings and his son, John Jr., operated the brewery until the father's death in 1894.

From 1894 until 1903 the brewery was dormant. Then German-born Antone Castel, a longtime Klamath Falls businessman, purchased the brewery. He remodeled and enlarged the plant, adding a bottling works, and advertised "Good local lager beer, in bottles and kegs." Castel's Klamath Falls Brewery closed in 1912.

LA GRANDE

There was one brewery in La Grande, and it belonged to Julius Roesch from beginning to end. *Bräumeister* Roesch built a large

The original Julius Roesch Brewery, built in La Grande in 1885.

Brewery workers on the loading dock at the La Grande Brewery.

brick building in the 1100 block of Jefferson Avenue in 1885, soon enlarging it into a massive three-story structure that dwarfed the other buildings on the street. Here Roesch brewed a lager with the name "La Grande's Best."

Roesch was an innovative, skillful marketer, and his beer was shipped by wagon and rail to much of eastern Oregon. After thirty years of continuous beer production, the La Grande Brewery finally succumbed, not to competition, but to Oregon's statewide prohibition in 1916.

LAKEVIEW

This south-central Oregon ranching community had one longtime brewery, although two others started and failed. The Lakeview Brewery was established in 1886 by brothers W. M. and

La Grande Brewery beer was delivered locally by wagon, in this photo to R. Kelley's Oregon Bar. Roesch also shipped his beer by freight wagon and rail to much of eastern Oregon and Idaho.

A. W. Goos. They built a modest wooden building for their kettle and vats at the end of Water Street (now North E Street).

After two years the Goos brothers sold the brewery to an experienced brewer named George Jammerthal. He built up a lively trade and in 1893 expanded the brewery into a large two-story wooden structure at the same location. He also built the Brewery Saloon, attached to his Water Street brewhouse.

In 1896 Jammerthal sold the business to N. P. Tonningsen and his partner, Ayers. By early 1900, Ayers had acquired the entire business and had a new partner named Schlegal.

The Ayers and Schlegal Lakeview Brewery, with its experienced staff and reputation for fine local lager, greeted the new century at full speed. But in May of that year an uncontrollable fire, that demon of wooden frontier towns, swept through Lakeview, completely destroying all but two commercial buildings. The brewery was not one of the two.

With a community spirit common to small towns in those days, the entire business district, including the Lakeview Brewery, was rebuilt and going by October. The new brewery was a large, gleaming white one-story building with "Lakeview Brewery" painted across the top of its high false front. Ayers and Schlegal advertised the opening of the new brewery and also the comfort and convenience of their brewery saloon, featuring that delectable custom of early-day taverns, the "free lunch." (See Interlude II: The Saloons for more on that delightful and long-gone tradition.)

The Lakeview Brewery continued under the same ownership for twelve more years, closing in 1912.

There were two false starts at opening competing breweries, but neither became established. In 1889 N. A. Clark tried to get a new brewery going, but by 1890 he was closed. Also in 1889, O. L. Stanley was licensed to operate a brewery, but there is no record of beer production, and in 1890 he did not reapply.

McMINNVILLE

In 1878 and 1879 Anton Ahrens and W. R. Bachman were partners in the small McMinnville Brewery. Ahrens also had a brewery in nearby St. Paul in the mid-1870s. A German brewer named Hermann Rehfuss and a man named Kolb purchased the small building and equipment in 1879. They advertised that their beer would be "delivered anywhere in the county free," and sold lager in kegs and bottles to a modest local clientele. Rehfuss and Kolb sold the brewery to Isadore Ertle in 1882, a brewer from Oregon City, and the new owner produced lager and porter until the end of 1886.

MEDFORD

Beer was first brewed in Medford in 1893 at the Southern Oregon Brewery & Ice Works, located on the northwest corner of Fourth and Fir Streets. The owner was G. W. Blasford. Elias Merc acquired the plant in 1897 and changed the name to Medford Brewing Company. Henry Weinhard, the Portland beer magnate, purchased the brewery in 1902. He found it economically sound to close the brewery and use the facilities as a receiving and storage depot for his beer brewed in Portland. Thus for some years the Medford brewery was known officially as the Medford Agency, Henry Weinhard Co. of Portland.

After Prohibition was repealed in 1933, the old Medford brewery was one of the few in the state to reopen. It was purchased by a group of investors who remodeled and modernized the old ghost and christened it the Southern Oregon Brewing Company, Inc.

In 1938 the name was changed to A-One Brewing Co., and the general manager was Bill Chrysler. The name was changed once more, in 1945, to the Chrystal Brewing and Distributing Company, with Chrysler still in charge. They brewed "Chrystal Beer," and also brewed under the "King Cole" and "A-1" labels. Chrystal Brewing closed its doors in 1947. The Fourth and Fir site is now an outside storage yard, and only the front steps and part of the foundation of the old brewery still remain.

MERGANSER

Merganser was the name of a town that existed for ten years. It was located about two miles below Klamath Falls (then Linkville), in the area of the Highway 97 bridge. In 1884 Paul Breistenstein opened a brewery in a small house in Merganser. He closed it in 1886.

Paul Breistenstein's little brewery, pictured here in 1884, was located in the community of Merganser, near Klamath Falls. The brewery operated from 1884 to 1886.

MONUMENT

Here is a mysterious one. In a craft where few women ventured, Mary C. Allen founded a brewery in 1900 on her own in this Grant County community. Unfortunately, the details of her story have been lost in time, but by the end of 1901 her brewery was no more.

NEWPORT

From 1882 until 1897, happy, rotund Robert Schwaibold brewed a popular lager from a small wooden building on a knoll overlooking Yaquina Bay. Born in Germany, this likable brewmaster came to America when he was twenty-seven years old, already an experienced brewer. He worked at breweries in Cleveland and Omaha before moving to the Oregon coast in 1881. By the spring of the next year, Robert had built his Yaquina Brewery and was, as a contemporary writer put it, "supplying the surrounding country with good, wholesome beer." He continued to do so for fifteen years.

Robert Schwaibold, right, and his family pose in front of their Yaquina Brewery at Newport. Photo circa 1885.

Charlie Thom's Coos Bay Brewing Company in North Bend.

NORTH BEND

Charlie Thom's Coos Bay Brewing Company was located on Stanton Avenue near the water's edge of the bay for which it was named. Charlie built his four-story brewery in 1907. His chief competitor for the first few years was Robert Marsden's brewery, just up the road in the neighboring city of Marshfield (Coos Bay).

Thom was an immediate success, employing all the modern brewing and marketing techniques known to turn-of-the-century brewers. By 1911 he had constructed a concrete bottling works next to the brewery. This white building still stands as the home of the Bay Ice Company. Although excellent city water was available, Charlie had his own well dug, ensuring that only the purest water of the highest quality would be used in his "Coos Bay" and "Pacific Pride" beer, as well as his ice-making plant.

In 1916, when Oregon's state prohibition law put all breweries out of business, Charlie Thom emptied the brewkettle for the last time and closed the doors to one of North Bend's early successes.

OAKLAND

John Gottlieb Mehl opened the first brewery in the Douglas County farming community of Oakland, north of Roseburg, in 1872. Mehl built the Oakland Brewery soon after a fire destroyed his and partner John Rast's Roseburg Brewery. Gottlieb brewed beer in Oakland until 1877, then moved to the coast to open the Coquille City Brewery.

A. D. Robinson acquired the Oakland Brewery in 1877, but sold it the next year to John A. Fryer and Peter McGregor. In an unusual turnabout, McGregor bought out his partner in 1879, but the very next year John Fryer bought the brewery back from McGregor. Fryer continued brewing until 1887.

OREGON CITY

Oregon City, "at the end of the Oregon Trail," was in 1851 the first incorporated city west of the Rockies. The earliest brewery here was owned by Louis Behren from about 1858 to 1862, though no details are available.

In 1862 Henry Humbel began operating his Oregon City Brewery, and he was adept at obtaining free advertising. In the January 5, 1867 Oregon City *Enterprise,* the editor made public his appreciation of the brewer: "We can say, in thanks to Mr. Humbel, the proprietor of the Oregon City Brewery, that the keg of lager beer left at our office the day before New Year's is No. 1. We recommend it and numerous of our friends who have tried it do the same. No one need send out of the city now for a capital article of lager."

Henry Humbel had Jacob Mader as a partner by 1877, and their newspaper ads proclaimed:

Oregon City Brewery
Humbel & Mader, Props.
The Best Lager in Oregon

From 1877 through 1879, Hermann Rehfuss also had an interest in the brewery. In '79 he left to build his own brewery in the Willamette Valley at McMinnville. The Oregon City Brewery sold 1,412 barrels of beer in 1878.

In late 1879, Jacob Mader bought out Humbel's interest and ran the brewery as Jacob Mader's Oregon City Brewery until he sold it to Listman and Company in 1890. The old brewery was sold once again in 1891 to George Hartmann, and it was finally closed in 1894.

PENDLETON

Adolph Lang's Umatilla Brewery, built in 1878 at "W. Railroad Street, corner of Willow," was the first of four breweries established in this historic ranching and wheat center. Frank Arnold bought the brewery in 1884, and then came a succession of owners: B. Schmeer in 1888; R. Lambrecht in 1890; and Adam and Anton Nolte from 1891 to 1899.

The final owner of the Umatilla Brewery was a unique brewer from Belgium named Polydore Moens, who acquired the plant in 1899. Polydore learned the art of brewing at his father's brewery in the Old Country. A university graduate who spoke five languages, Moens landed in Pendleton in 1890. He first established himself as a market gardener. He also bought horses and shipped them to markets in Belgium.

When Moens bought the Umatilla Brewery, he remodeled it and increased the production to 60 barrels of lager per week. He closed the brewery to pursue other business interests in 1904.

Adam Stang started a brewery in Pendleton in 1878, and in 1879 he took on as his partner John B. Natter, the brewer from Albany, Portland, and Heppner. (See story on J. B. Natter in Heppner section.) In 1880 Natter bought out Mr. Stang and ran the brewery until 1884, when he closed it to give full attention to his other brewing enterprise in Heppner.

The brewery in business the longest in Pendleton, and the one most local people refer to when speaking of the "old Pendleton brewery," was William Roesch's operation, which ran from 1882 to 1947.

William Roesch, a brewer from Germany, owned a brewery in Heppner in 1881–82. He sold the business and moved to Pendleton, where he started the City Brewery in 1882 on Southeast Court Street. He was a popular and generous fellow, always ready to donate kegs of his finest lager for civic events.

Roesch conducted his brewery until forced to close by the state prohibition law, which took effect in January 1916.

In 1934, following repeal of the Volstead Act, the copper brewkettle was again fired up, still under Roesch family management.

A new structure had been built at 300-302 Southeast Court, next to the original site, and the old plant became the Roesch Bottling Works. Three popular Roesch brands were "Elk Horn," "Old Master," and "Western Club Special." The Roesch Brewing Co. continued to turn out lager beer for Oregon's wheat-belt folks for another ten years. The brewery finally closed in 1947 after a total of 47 years in business.

The fourth brewery in Pendleton was a small operation owned by Henry Schultz from 1897 until 1910.

PORTLAND

From the time of its founding in 1845, Oregon's largest city has been home to 23 breweries (including six recent microbreweries).

Liberty Brewery. Henry Saxer started things off in the Pacific Northwest when he opened his Liberty Brewery in 1852 near what is now First and Davis Streets in Portland. Eight years later his original small wooden house had grown to three large adjoining two-story buildings.

In 1862 Saxer sold his brewery to a young German brewer named Henry Weinhard from neighboring Fort Vancouver,

Henry Saxer's Liberty Brewery, Portland, in the early 1860s, as it looked when young Henry Weinhard bought it.

across the Columbia River. Thus began the epoch of Oregon's largest and longest-running brewing company. The highlights of this interesting and historic Northwest enterprise can be found in Chapter Five.

Over the years, Portland's other breweries competed with varying degrees of success for a share of the beer market.

East Portland Brewery. Located at present-day Union Avenue and Southeast Washington Street, the East Portland Brewery was established in 1870 by Henry Ludwig. He advertised lager, beer, ale, and porter in kegs and bottles. In 1878 Ludwig sold the brewery to Henry Humbel of Oregon City and John Kroetz. Lambert Kratz was the proprietor in 1882, and he closed the brewery in 1884.

Jubitz and Scheland Brewery. Partners A. Jubitz and Scheland owned small breweries from 1874 to 1876. Little is known of these brief ventures, not even the exact locations.

Gambrinus Brewery. Built in 1875 by Louis Feurer, the Gambrinus Brewery was a large, well-known operation taking up four blocks in the area of 22nd and Flanders. Feurer sold 1,089 barrels of lager in 1879. The facility was moved to 793 Washington in 1892, and when the plant opened at its new location Louis Feurer placed this ad in the *Oregonian*:

GAMBRINUS BEER
is a mild, healthful
beverage. Gambrinus Beer
refreshes, nourishes and gives
strength to reconvalescence,
therefore it is recommended
by all doctors in this
Northwestern country.
Office, Washington Street,
opposite City Park, Portland.

After twenty years of brewing, Louis Feurer sold the plant in 1895 to George Leithof. The brewery was closed by state and later federal Prohibition in 1916. In 1934 a new owner, Theodore J. Schmidt, reopened with a modern facility at a new location, 817 Northeast Madrona, and under a new name, Rose City Brewing Co. The brewery closed in 1940, but the building still stands as the Grigsby Bros. paper box factory.

U. S. BREWERY,

HERRALL & ZIMMERMAN, Proprietors.

We have the Latest Improvements, use the Very Best Materials, and are prepared to furnish the Public with the Finest Quality of

LAGER BEER.

COR. WATER AND HARRISON STS.,

PORTLAND, - - - OREGON.

The United States Brewing Co. produced beer in Portland from 1873 to 1896 in its plant on the east bank of the Willamette River.

United States Brewing Co. This brewery was established in 1873 on the west side of Front Street, between Clay and Columbia. George Herrall, a brewer from Baden in southwest Germany, built the beer plant and first called it the Eagle Brewery. In 1876 the name was changed to U.S. Brewery.

The U.S. Brewery sold 1,506 barrels of lager in 1878. The next year Herrall moved the brewery to Harrison and Water Streets in East Portland. Here he constructed an imposing four-story brewing plant and residence. George Herrall's beer sold well, and in time he had sales agents as far south as San Diego, and north to Canada. The brewery closed with his death in 1896.

Belinger-Weiss Brewery. The modest Belinger-Weiss Brewery was located at the northeast corner of Northeast Ninth and East

Couch Streets from 1877 to 1879. The plant was acquired by Molson & Sons in 1879 and operated under their name until 1882. It was purchased in that year by Diesing & Neunert, who ran it until 1884.

South Portland Brewery. Joseph Weber's South Portland Brewery was in business from 1882 to 1885 at South First between Gibbs and Grover, about where the Barbur interchange is now located.

Schaefer & Burelbach. Schaefer & Burelbach had a short-lived brewing enterprise from 1886 to 1887. The brewery location is unknown.

Britannia Brewing Co. This brewery held forth on the northwest corner of Eighth and Washington in East Portland in 1886. No other information is available.

Wilhelm Brewery. Also known as Sellwood Brewery, this beer plant in the Sellwood district of Portland was owned by John G. Wilhelm from 1893 until his death in 1902. After the old brewmaster's passing, his wife Mary kept the brewery running until 1904.

With the arrival of railroads, Northwest breweries faced increasing competition from large companies to the east. This 1905 photo shows a load of St. Louis beer stopped in front of the Fountain Saloon at Second and Washington Streets in Portland.

The Wilhelm Brewery had an attached saloon and was located on the northwest corner of Ninth and Marion Streets. In 1899 John had a partner named Benedict Bermoser, who looked after the company's second saloon at 216 Front Street in downtown Portland.

Some of the structure of the old Sellwood Brewery still stands today as part of Kinco International's "Fratelli's Ice Cream" plant.

Portland Weissbeer Brewing and Bottling Co. This small brewery stood at 537 Milwaukie from 1902 to 1904, when new owners changed the name to Deter & Co. The brewery closed in 1907. It specialized in *Weissbier,* a light, whitish Bavarian beer that has no strong hops or malt flavor, but is generally tart and lively. It is usually brewed from wheat.

Portland Brewing Company. Arnold Blitz, of later Blitz-Weinhard fame, conducted the Portland Brewing Company at 1991 Upshur. From 1904 until 1916 the plant brewed "Edel Bräu" lager beer. When state prohibition emptied the brewkettle in 1916, Arnold Blitz made nonalcoholic drinks and syrups. The famous Blitz-Weinhard merger was made in 1928, and following

In 1908 Arnold Blitz, second from left, and his Portland Brewing Company crew made "Edel Bräu" brand beer.

Brass advertising plaque from Portland's Mt. Hood Brewing Co., 1905–1913. It now hangs on a wall in "The Brewery" in Grants Pass.

Repeal the Upshur plant was used as an adjunct brewing facility of Blitz-Weinhard until 1940. The old Portland Brewing Co. building still stands as today's Point Adams Packing Company.

Enterprise Brewing Co. From 1905 to 1911 the Enterprise Brewing Company was in business at North 13th and Johnson.

Mt. Hood Brewing Co. Located on East Water Street between Hawthorne and Madison, this brewery ran from 1905 to 1913. No brewery structure remains.

North Pacific Brewing Co. This was the Portland branch brewery of John Kopp's main operation in Astoria. The brewery was at 18th and Upshur from 1905 to 1911. There was a downtown sales office at 211 McKay Building.

Cartwright Brewing Co. This was a small brewery lasting from 1980 to 1982 at 617 Southeast Main.

PRAIRIE CITY

Otto Mahl had a brewery in this Grant County community from 1880 to 1890. Also, from 1889 to 1891 Paul Fieman ran a small brewery and saloon.

PRINEVILLE

There were two breweries in this central Oregon ranching town. The Ochoco Brewery, a small one-story, false-front building on the main street, was started in 1882 by Frank Locher and a partner named Solomon. In 1884 Locher sold the Ochoco to Asa Miles and Evans, who owned it for another six years. The Ochoco Brewery closed in 1890.

Prineville's other brewery, also a modest wooden structure, was built in 1893 by S. W. Woods, who called it the City Brewery. Within several years it was sold to the O'Neil brothers, George and Walter, who ran it until 1906.

RANDOLPH

Joseph Walser, an Austrian-born brewer, built a brewery in Randolph in 1883. The tiny settlement of sixty people could hardly have supported a brewery, but the location on the north bank of the Coquille River was ideal for shipping by waterway to nearby Coquille City, Bandon, and Marshfield (Coos Bay), as well as to all the small coal-mining settlements in the area.

The capacity of the brewery in 1884 was 300 barrels per month, although the actual production was less than half that. Walser's "Randolph Beer" was popular for a number of years until the brewery closed in 1891.

In that year Herr Walser went to California to ply his trade, but returned to Coos County in 1895. He purchased the Bandon Brewery from Gottlieb Mehl's widow in 1896 and operated it until 1900.

ROSEBURG

There were two breweries in Roseburg. The first one was established by John Gottlieb Mehl in 1861.

Gottlieb Mehl, a German-born brewer who crossed the plains

John Rast (seated with cane by the tree) and part of the crew of Rast's Roseburg Brewery relax as they display their product. Note the different styles of beer glasses and the keg on the chair.

to Oregon in 1849, was an early settler in Douglas (then Umpqua) County. He filed a Donation Land Claim near present Roseburg in 1851, and by 1861 was brewing lager beer on Deer Creek in his Roseburg Brewery.

In 1866 *Bräumeister* Mehl took a partner named John G. Rast, a 28-year-old Swiss immigrant who had also learned the brewing trade. The Mehl and Rast brewery malted its own barley and brewed with excellent water from a nearby spring.

A fire on January 10, 1871 destroyed a large part of the brewery, and later that month Gottlieb Mehl sold his interest in the business to Rast. By May 1872 Mehl had opened another brewery twenty miles to the north in Oakland. He would build two more breweries, at Coquille City and Bandon, before his death in 1893.

John Rast, meanwhile, rebuilt the damaged Roseburg Brewery and continued as the town's only brewer. In an interview years later, John V. Rast, son of the brewer, recalled the days growing up at his father's brewery. He remembered that water from the spring ran by gravity flow to an 8-by-12-foot redwood tank in the brewery. An old horse circled endlessly around a sweep, grinding the malted barley used in the beer.

The younger Rast also remembered good times at the saloon attached to his father's brewery. "Quite a crowd were regular patrons there," he told an interviewer. "In addition to beer, crackers and cheese were offered, also jerky. Men gathered here, an accordion furnished music, and there was singing, music, and good fellowship."

John Rast died from an accident in 1898, and his widow closed the brewery. The old building was used as a warehouse for years until it was torn down in the 1920s. Today nothing remains to mark the site, at Diamond Lake Boulevard and Stephens, of one of Roseburg's earliest and most successful businesses.

Roseburg's second brewery, Roseburg Brewing and Ice Co., was owned by Max Weiss in 1899. Weiss learned the brewing art in his father's brewery in Germany. Arriving in America in 1886, Herr Weiss worked at breweries in Philadelphia, Cincinnati, Michigan, California, and British Columbia. In 1898 he came to Roseburg, bought out the ice company, and remodeled the building into an enormous brewery covering an entire city block.

Exterior view of Max Weiss's Roseburg Brewing & Ice Co., prior to 1906.

The Oregon Saloon in Grants Pass featured "Roseburg Beer" just after the turn of the century.

In 1901 Max installed a bottling machine with a capacity of 200 bottles per hour. His label read "Roseburger Export Beer." With business jumping, the next year Weiss increased his brewing capacity from 15 barrels a day to 52. He also established sales agents in southern Oregon at Ashland and Grants Pass, and on the coast. The August 18, 1902 issue of the Roseburg *Plaindealer* declared: "It is needless to say that Max Weiss is producing a beverage which is second to none on the Pacific Coast."

Max Weiss sold his brewery in 1905 to a group of investors from Portland for $50,000. He stayed in Roseburg until 1912, when he purchased a brewery in Ukiah, California.

The beer brewing business was finished at Roseburg in 1908 when the county went "dry" under the local option law. Roseburg Brewing & Ice Co. made a near beer drink for some years, and emphasized the manufacture and sales of ice. In 1914 the company had a contract with Southern Pacific to serve as a major icing station for refrigerated railroad cars. The contract required the old brewery to maintain a ready supply of 1,000 tons of block ice.

The site of the Roseburg Brewing & Ice Co. is on Short Street, between Burke and Sykes, along the railroad tracks.

Two other attempts to start breweries were made in Roseburg over the years, though neither was successful. In 1878–79, Thomas F. Kreuztscher was licensed to operate a brewery, though no production was recorded. David Meyer and Leonard Schmitt had a small brewery to serve their own saloon from 1895 to 1896.

ST. PAUL

Anton Ahrens, a brewer from nearby McMinnville, had a small brewery in St. Paul from 1875 to 1879. He produced 94 barrels of beer in 1878 and 83 barrels in 1879.

SALEM

Oregon's capital city had two breweries, and both were established in 1866. Samuel Adolph was brewing at Church and Trade Streets, and Louis Westacott made beer in his Pioneer Brewery at the foot of Mission Street.

Samuel Adolph arrived at Salem in 1862, and four years later had the finances to open his own brewery and put to use the skills he had learned in Germany. He chose a location on the south side of Trade Street, between Cottage and Church. Soon the Pacific Brewery was making lager beer to help supply the thirteen saloons in town.

In 1869, a fire destroyed the brewery. Adolph moved three blocks west to the southeast corner of Trade and Commercial. There he built a new brewery, naming it the Salem Brewery. He brewed in this location for the next sixteen years.

Adolph sold the plant in 1885 to Maurice Klinger and Seraphin Beck, brewery employees, who later bought the property across Trade Street on the northeast corner. They constructed a building 75 × 80 feet and produced 3,500 barrels of beer per year. The new operation was called the Capital Brewery. It had an attached saloon—with sawdust floor, 5¢ beer, and free lunch—which reputedly was a popular place for businessmen, legislators, and jurists.

The Capital Brewery was sold in 1903 to Leopold Schmidt of the Olympia Brewing Co. One of his sons, Frank Schmidt, and the Olympia business manager, Frank M. Kenney, together with Kola Neis, managed what was now known as the Salem Brewery Association. The plant was enlarged in 1910 to include an immense four-story building. The brewery used one million pounds

This 1934 bottle of "Salem Beer" was one of the first produced after Prohibition. The beer was made by the Salem Brewery Association, owned by Olympia Brewing Company of Tumwater, Washington.

of hops per year to produce the celebrated "Salem Beer," sold from southern California to Alaska. The brewmasters were Charles Scholl, Leo Schmidt, and Paul Schmidt.

When Prohibition was repealed in 1933, the Salem Brewery Association plant was reactivated, and continued brewing "Salem Beer" for another ten years.

In 1943 the brewery was purchased by Emil G. Sick of the Sicks' Seattle Brewing & Malting Co., and the name was changed to Sicks' Brewing Co. Under the guidance of manager Floyd Shepard and brewmaster Steve Tabacci, Sicks' Brewery produced 100,000 barrels of beer annually, including the popular "Sicks' Select" and "Brew 66." They also made "Brown Derby" beer for

Safeway Stores, Inc. The Salem facility closed in 1953, and Sicks' concentrated its output at its enlarged breweries in Seattle and Spokane.

English-born Louis Westacott started his brewery in 1866 not far from Adolph's, and for sixteen years the two friends were spirited competitors. Louis Westacott's location was at the west end of Mission Street, then called Sleepy Hollow, about where present Mission and Saginaw Streets cross. Since Westacott arrived at Salem in 1851, eleven years earlier than Adolph, he called his new brewery the Pioneer Brewery.

Although the Englishman may have been fond of his country's ales and porter, the Pioneer Brewery was strictly a lager operation. He used horsepower to run the pumps, malt mill, and other machinery. In 1870 he enlarged his building and converted to steam power.

W. G. Westacott, Louis's son, joined his father in the business from 1879 to 1882. The father's ill health forced the brewery to close in 1882, and Louis died in 1889.

This view of the Salem Brewery Association plant looks west on Trade Street, circa 1940.

By 1949 the Salem Brewery was owned by Emil G. Sick of Seattle's Rainier Brewing Co. This 1949 magazine advertisement boasted first prize for the "Sicks' Select" beer label in a national brewing industry "beautiful label" contest.

SCOTTSBURG

L. H. Rumelhart started a small brewery in this Douglas County community in 1878. The October 11, 1878 edition of the Roseburg *Western Star* announced: "L. H. Rumelhart has established a new brewery at Scottsburg, and hereafter the people of that community will be supplied with a delicious article of beer of home manufacture."

There was a curious twist to the story, however, because in the same issue of the *Western Star* was this item: "L. H. Rumelhart and

Jos. Hunt were arrested at Scottsburg last Tuesday by Deputy U.S. Marshal Burns, on a charge of selling beer and cigars without license. They were taken to Portland Wednesday for trial."

Perhaps L. H. began selling his "delicious article of beer" a bit too soon. In any event, his brewery was short-lived and closed by the end of 1879.

SUMMERVILLE

George Ott ran a brewery in this Wallowa County town from 1886 until 1910.

SUMPTER

Sumpter had a multi-owned brewery of short duration from 1899 to 1905. John Rohrman, a brewer from Burns, built the brewery. He sold it in 1902 and moved to Joseph, where he opened another one. The Sumpter operation, doing business as Columbia Brewing and Malting Co., was acquired by A. W. Ellis and a partner named Zizelman. They ran the brewery until 1905, when they closed it.

THE DALLES

There were two breweries in this historic town on the Columbia River. The first one was established by Emile Schanno in 1874. Little information is available about his brewery, but it is known that in 1875 he sold out to R. O. Porak, who continued the business until 1884.

The best known brewery in The Dalles was established in 1876 by August Buchler. His Columbia Brewery was located at 906 East Second, at the bottom of what is now called Brewery Grade. *Bräumeister* Buchler, who learned his trade in the Old Country, made lager and porter, and in 1879 produced 881 barrels of it. His chief competition came from Portland's Weinhard and Gambrinus breweries, but his products were proudly featured in area saloons. The Oro Fino Saloon, for example, advertised the "Celebrated Columbia Beer on draught" and a splendid free lunch to go along with it. August also had a saloon at 601 East Second, near the brewery.

In 1905 the aging Buchler sold his brewery, and the new owners changed the name to Eastern Oregon Brewing Co. It remained in operation until 1916.

UNION

In 1868 Charles F. Schoppe operated the Schoppe Brewery in Union. Eleven years later, in 1879, S. N. Washburn had a small brewery. He sold it that same year to Henry Stickler and Jacob Zuber, who ran it for five years.

UTTER CITY

George Stauf, a brewer from nearby Marshfield (Coos Bay), owned a brewery in this tiny coal-mining settlement from 1875 to 1876, when the mines closed and so did the brewery.

WESTON

Thomas Berry had a modest brewery in this Umatilla County community from 1882 until 1885.

WALDO

Waldo was a gold-mining town near the Illinois River in southern Oregon. Joseph Marhoffer and Randall Sanns owned a brewery there in the 1860s and early 1870s—the dates are vague in existing records. The partners' main brewery was in Crescent City, California, where they were in the trade from 1857 to 1888. The Waldo Brewery appears to have been strictly a keg beer operation to supply the saloons and mines in the district.

WILDERVILLE

David Closner had a small brewery in this Josephine County town from 1879 to 1880. In 1879 he sold seventeen barrels of beer.

Interlude One

The Infamous 18th Amendment

ARTICLE XVIII

1. NATIONAL PROHIBITION. *After one year from the ratification of this article, the manufacture, sale, or transportation of intoxicating liquors within, the importation thereof into, or the exportation thereof from the United States and all territory subject to the jurisdiction thereof for beverage purposes is hereby prohibited.*

BY THE TIME THE 18TH Amendment was added to the U.S. Constitution, effective January 16, 1920, Oregon and Washington had already been "dry" for four years by popular vote. Even as far back as the 1840s, influential prohibitionists among certain religious and political leaders in the Oregon Country had made their views known with varying degrees of success.

In 1844, for example, the manufacture and sale of "ardent spirits" was made illegal in the Pacific Northwest by the provisional government at Oregon City. Five years later, in the first legislative session of the New Oregon Territory, a bill was passed allowing the manufacture of liquor, but imposing heavy license fees and taxes on the makers and sellers. The law also provided that no saloon, distillery, or other commercial enterprise could "sell, barter, or give away" any kind of spiritous beverage to Indians, under penalty of a $100 fine.

During the 1850s and '60s, the prohibitionist movement, through societies such as the Sons of Temperance, lobbied for laws that would rout out "whiskey mongers" and "tippling-house keepers." In 1854 a prohibition petition was signed by 74 people who wanted to succeed "in making our beautiful country a country that knoweth not the 'worm of the still'." But since most of the population in the Oregon Territory did not go along with the idea, the prohibitionists attracted little attention.

With the added support, however, of the national Prohibition Party, organized in 1869, and the Women's Christian Temperance Union, a strict prohibition measure was put on the ballot in the 1887 Oregon state election. It was defeated by almost 3-to-1. Seventeen years passed before another prohibition measure was placed on the ballot.

Meanwhile, Washington had gained statehood in 1889, and when the constitution of the new state was submitted to voters a prohibition clause was soundly defeated.

In 1904 scattered pockets of the temperance movement were revived, with firm help from a strengthened W.C.T.U. and the Anti-Saloon League, and carried to success a local option law in Oregon, with Washington following in 1909. Under local option, counties held their own elections to determine whether they would go "dry" or "wet." With the inconsistent popularity of the prohibitionist philosophy, some counties voted "dry" while neighboring counties remained "wet." You could buy beer in Douglas County, Oregon, for example, but not across the line in Coos County.

To make matters even more confusing, during this tme there were "home rule" laws that also affected the manufacture and sale of beer and other liquor. Under home rule, cities within the same county could enact their own local liquor prohibition laws, regardless of the county ordinances. Thus, in 1910, no one could buy beer in the city of Eugene, Oregon, though it was legal to do so in the neighboring town of Springfield—both in Lane County, which was "dry." In fact, the tiny mill community of Springfield, right across the Willamette River from Eugene, was quite an attraction between 1910 and 1913. Hundreds of Eugene residents regularly paid 6¢ to ride the streetcar over the bridge to reach the saloons along Springfield's Main Street. By 1912 Springfield had more drinking emporiums than churches. Similar "wet" versus "dry" situations were found all over the Pacific Northwest during the early years of this century.

But in 1914 there came a turnabout, with the prohibitionists gaining support and influence in the legislatures of both Oregon and Washington. They wanted the two states purged of liquor, and with a great expenditure of money the "drys" began to prevail. It was quite a fight. Elections on the issue were coming up in each state. The prohibitionists enlisted such notables as the famed preacher "Billy" Sunday to stump through Oregon and Washington extolling the virtues of life without spiritous beverages, including beer.

The "wets," backed by the considerable resources of the large brewers and others in the liquor industry, hired Clarence Darrow to speak on the value of free choice and reasonable laws; laws that allowed the controlled and taxed manufacture and sale of fermented and distilled liquids.

The prohibitionists carried the day in the November 3, 1914 elections in Washington and Oregon: both states were voted "dry." One chief factor in that surprising outcome was the vote of women, who had gained voting rights two years before. It is estimated that three out of every four women who voted chose prohibition.

Appropriate amendments were drafted into the states' constitutions, and prohibition arrived in Oregon and Washington on January 1, 1916.

An amusing feature of the rush to lay in beer and other liquor before the New Year's closure was the number of avowed prohibitionists who sought to get in a little nip for themselves. As reported in the Portland *Oregonian,* one dour gentleman, who said he would under no circumstances drink anything alcoholic himself, bought ten gallons of beer for use as "hair tonic."

The breweries of the Pacific Northwest turned off their brew-kettles and closed their doors, many never to reopen. The brewers gave away much of the final batches of beer to their communities for last-day parties. Portland's 400 saloons were busy that last night, as were Seattle's 750 drinking emporiums. Most of them ran out of all liquor, including beer, by around 8 p.m. on December 31, 1915. It was to be a long dry spell.

National Prohibition

Throughout the early years of this century, the prohibitionist movement gained ground across the nation. It arose from the sincere belief of many Americans, mostly white Protestants whose ancestors were pioneer settlers, that the drinking of alcoholic beverages, especially among the millions of newly arrived immigrants in the cities, was a threat to law and order. There was some evidence to support that belief: drunkenness in the dense slums of large cities was a factor in rowdyism and crime.

By 1917 the prohibitionists had already induced 25 states to pass "dry" laws. In 1919 three-fourths of the states ratified an amendment to the U.S. Constitution, the eighteenth, that forbade all manufacturing, selling, and transportation of intoxicating liquors in the United States. Congress, also in 1919, passed the Volstead Act, which established penalties for violation of the 18th Amendment.

Prohibition went into effect in this country on the morning of January 16, 1920, and at once thousands of Americans began to disobey it, defying the new law because they thought it violated their right to live according to their own standards. Many families and working men in the Pacific Northwest, as elsewhere, enjoyed beer as a beverage, not as a means to intoxication.

Soon little stores called "malt shops" began opening up across the land. They sold malt (fortunately still legal because of its use in baking) and other things, the uses of which were not hard to divine: bottle caps, yeast, and even beer mugs. Home brewing became common in the cellars, garages, and back rooms of American homes. Amateur brewers soon became experts, and few social gatherings of that period were complete without long discussions of brewing techniques, particularly the right time to pour the beer from crock to bottle. If bottled too soon, it was likely to explode, and on bad nights whole city blocks sounded like battlefields.

The home brewer didn't have to be an expert to turn out a line of potent potables for personal use. One enterprising mail-order firm offered a malt concoction that carried the inviting warning: "Do not add yeast to this product since that will create alcohol, which is illegal." There are reports that a number of people did.

National Prohibition was a failure almost from the beginning. Enforcement was difficult and haphazard, and it gave rise to crooked politicians and enforcement officers. Underworld gangs started supplying huge quantities of alcoholic beverages in many cities and towns. Smuggling was rampant, expecially along the northern tier states. Canada ended its national prohibition in 1919, and millions of gallons of hard liquor and beer were brought illegally over the line to the U.S. The value of Canadian-smuggled liquor in 1924 alone totaled over forty million dollars.

Refreshments of Pure Delight **WEINHARD'S**

R-PORTER
True Raspberry Flavor
APPO
Pure Apple Cider
LUXO
The Cheery, Beery Drink
TOKO
True Loganberry Grape Flavor
Order WEINHARD'S PURITAN
brand pure fruit flavored carbonated beverages by the case.
All Flavors—Straight or Assorted
Special Allowance for Return of Case and Bottles
Phone your dealer, or call
THE HENRY WEINHARD PLANT
Broadway 383 PORTLAND, OREGON

During Prohibition, the Blitz-Weinhard Brewing Co. produced syrups, flavorings, and nonalcoholic fruit drinks. Advertisement circa 1929.

It was estimated that less than five percent of all illegal liquor flowing through the country ever fell into government hands. In Portland, officers confiscated 2,026 quarts of beer in July 1927. They believed that amount to be less than one-tenth of the illegal beer in the city that month.

While many Pacific Northwest breweries closed their doors for good, some stalwart brewers weathered the dry years by making nonalcoholic fruit beverages, syrups, and flavorings. Henry Weinhard made "R-PORTER," a raspberry drink; "APPO" apple cider; and "TOKO," a loganberry/grape-flavored beverage. Olympia produced "Applju" from apples, and a fruit drink called "Loju."

By the late 1920s, many Americans decided that Prohibition had brought more harm than good. Crime had increased, and enforcement was ineffective. The Great Depression, with its worldwide business slump, began in 1929. Many influential citizens thought Prohibition should end so that the government could again collect taxes and fees on alcoholic beverages to help stimulate the economy.

After thirteen years of virtual extinction, the American brewing industry came to life again in 1933. On March 21st Congress passed the Cullen Bill, which legalized the manufacture and sale of beer, to take effect on April 7th of that year. Repeal of the entire 18th Amendment followed on December 5, 1933.

Pacific Northwest breweries were reactivated, though many of the smaller operations lacked the resources to begin again. At first there was not enough beer to satisfy the tremendous demand, but soon the breweries were running at full capacity. Once again Americans could enjoy a glass of beer at home, in the neighborhood tavern, or at a community picnic in lawful relaxation. The dark days of Prohibition had come to an end.

Following Repeal, Blitz-Weinhard happily resumed brewing beer, as indicated in this 1934 magazine ad.

Chapter Four

Brewed in Washington

ASHINGTON'S 138 BREWERIES have worked to quench the beer thirst of loggers, fishermen, farmers, and other folks since 1854, when Nicholas Delin first started making beer in Steilacoom. Two of the original breweries are still in operation, and a number of new smaller ones are producing beer for a loyal following.

Most of the old-time breweries in the Evergreen State are long gone. But if you squint your mind's eye you can see wooden kegs stacked on a loading dock, smoke rolling from the tall brewery stacks, and thirsty businessmen heading for the "commodious saloon attached."

Here are the breweries of Washington.

ABERDEEN

There were two breweries in this lumber and fishing port. The earliest attempt to start a brewery was made by L. Blum and H. E. Anderson in 1889, in a small structure on Wilson Creek, but little beer was made and by 1890 they were closed. The Grays Harbor Brewing Company, at River and Lincoln Streets, was built in 1900 by Seattle brewers Alvin and Elmer Hemrich.

Grays Harbor Brewing changed its name to Aberdeen Brewing Company in 1902. The plant produced lager beer in kegs and bottles to supply saloons and logging camps throughout the south coast of Washington until 1916.

In 1933, after the Dark Days, the old brewery was modernized and reactivated by the Hemrich interests. The name was now Pioneer Brewing Company, but it was still known to the old-timers as the Aberdeen Brewery. It was located at 408 South Lincoln

Elmer Hemrich, right, poses in front of the brewery with some of his Aberdeen Brewing Company crew and one of his beer delivery wagons in 1903.

Street, and there it produced beer into the 1950s. None of the brewery structure remains.

AUBURN

This King County railroad community had two breweries. The first was built in 1891 when Auburn was still called Slaughter. The Slaughter Brewing and Malting Company ran until 1897.

The other brewery in town was the Friend-Degginger Import Co., operating from 1893 to 1897.

BELLINGHAM

The earliest attempt at a brewery in Bellingham was in 1885, when J. Beck opened a small plant. He closed it two years later.

Fritz Grathwohl's Whatcom Brewing and Malting Co., on Iowa Street, was in business from 1899 to 1904. He closed it and moved to Oroville, Washington, where he started another brewery.

The main brewery in Bellingham was the Bellingham Bay Brewery. It was built in 1903 at Ellis and Ohio Streets by Leopold

Schmidt of the Olympia Brewing Company. The brewmaster was Henry Schupp.

Schmidt and Schupp developed innovative brewing equipment for the Bellingham plant, making it the third brewery in North America of its kind. Before this, the brewing process included fermenting in open vats, which exposed the beer to impurities in the air. The system used by the Bellingham Bay Brewery was a much more sterile process that protected the beer from contamination. From the time the beer was cooked in the brewkettle until it was on the market in kegs or bottles, not one drop came in contact with the air or outside influences, and all the fermentation took place under pressure in enclosed vats. Other breweries began using the procedure, and soon it was common.

In 1904 Fritz Grathwohl sold his Whatcom Brewing Co. to Leopold Schmidt, who combined it with the Bellingham Bay Brewery. The brewery had two 50-ton ice machines, capable of making enough ice to supply all of northern Washington. The plant had a capacity of 100,000 barrels per year, and it marketed beer in Washington, Alaska, San Francisco, British Columbia, the Hawaiian Islands, and the Orient.

In 1909 Leopold Schmidt sold the Bellingham Bay Brewery to Edward L. Stowe, who continued producing beer under the "3-B Beer" label until 1916. After Prohibition an attempt was made to reopen the brewery as the Whatcom-Skagit Brewing Company, but there is no record of beer production.

CHELAN FALLS

Charles A. Schindler and his son Charles Jr. owned the brewery known as Schindler & Son Brewing and Malting Co. in this upper Columbia River community from 1902 until 1910. Schindler the elder learned the trade in Germany, and when he came to America he worked for breweries in St. Louis, Cincinnati, and St. Paul. The Chelan Falls brewery had a capacity of 2,000 barrels a year.

CHENEY

Joseph Weber, a brewer from Portland, opened the Bavaria Brewery in 1884. Alois Schmidt acquired the brewery in 1907 and operated it until 1910.

Another brewery was built in 1884 by Frank Locher and Charles Jensen. Locher was from Prineville, Oregon, where he owned a brewery before he moved to Cheney. The Locher-Jensen plant, known as the City Brewery, was located on Railroad Street. It was in business until 1888.

CHESAW

Three partners, Krause, Clerff, and Wilkstrom, attempted to start a brewery in this Okanogan County village in 1900, but there is no record of beer production.

CHEWELAH

There was one brewery with a succession of owners in Chewelah. The Loaker & Delva Brewery, built in 1886, was sold four years later to Joseph Fox, who sold it to Engelbert Leible in 1893. Leible brewed beer for the Chewelah district of Stevens County for five years. Frank Ernst acquired the Chewelah Brewery in 1898 and operated it with a partner, Joseph Pohle of Colville, until it closed in 1912.

COLFAX

The brewery in Colfax was long in operation and long in its list of owners. It was built in 1878 as the Erford & Palmtag Brewery. In 1879 they sold 159 barrels of lager.

The brewery was destroyed in a devastating July 1882 fire that wiped out most of the business buildings in Colfax. Erford and his new partner Woolford rebuilt the brewery, and they sold it in 1888 to the Michaelson brothers. The brothers held it for two years and in 1890 sold it to Charles and Mary E. Bourgardes, who brewed under the name M. E. Bourgardes & Co., Brewery & Saloon.

In 1892 Alvin Schmidt bought the brewery and kept it longer than any other owner—ten years. He sold it to the Schultz Brewing Co. in 1902, and Schultz sold it to the final owner, Max Hoefle, who called it the Colfax Brewing and Malting Co. Max closed the old brewery in 1916 with the advent of state prohibition.

COLVILLE

John U. Hofstetter is a name well-known to those interested in the history of the Colville Valley, for he was the founder and first mayor of the city of Colville. He was also a brewer.

Born in the Old Country in 1829, Hofstetter came to the east

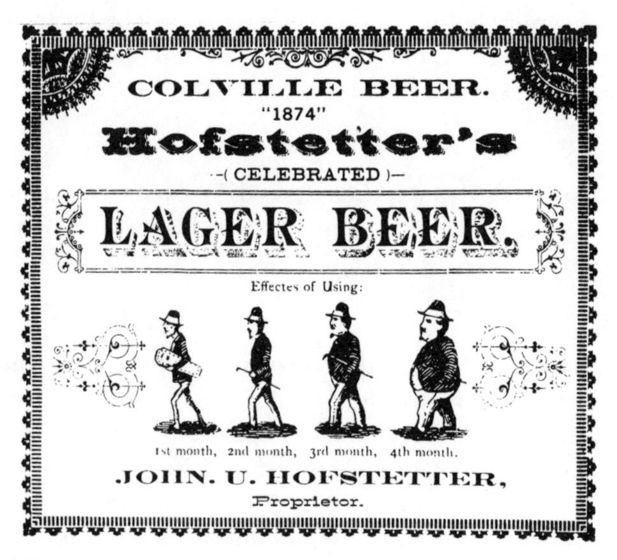

Colville brewer John U. Hofstetter's finest lager beer could make a weak man strong, according to this 1874 placard.

coast of America in 1854 and moved west four years later. In 1865, with a six-barrel copper brewkettle brought across the plains, he opened a small brewery in Pickney City near his homestead on the Colville River. A fire took the brewery in 1873, so the pioneer brewer packed his machinery and kettle four miles west to his homestead property. He erected a new brewery at the corner of Dominion and First Streets in his new town of Colville. At the Colville Brewery he sold keg beer and also ran an attached saloon. He sold 186 barrels of lager in 1879.

In 1890 Hofstetter sold the brewery to Andrew Schipps so he could focus his attention on his stock ranch and political life. Schipps held the brewery until 1892, selling it that year to Joseph Pohle. Pohle sold to Arnold Krueger in 1904.

Through this succession of owners the plant was continually called the Colville Brewery. In 1906 Krueger changed the name to Colville Brewing and Malting Co., and he closed the brewery in 1909.

Until September 1991, Colville was also the home of Hale's Ales, a microbrewery started in 1983 (see Chapter Six).

DAVENPORT

A small brewery was opened here in 1886 by A. Miltzer, but he closed it in 1887. The brewery was reopened in 1893 by Robert Tischner and a partner named Schultheis. They sold the brewery to W. A. Crawford in 1897, and by 1899 it was permanently closed.

DAYTON

Peter Rumpf and his partner, Dunkel, built the first Dayton Brewery in 1878. That year they sold 87 barrels of beer. Jacob Weinhard became a partner in 1879, and five years later he bought out Rumpf's interest. Jacob, the nephew of Portland brew king Henry Weinhard, operated the Dayton Brewery until 1900.

In 1880 Benjamin Scott, a brewer from Walla Walla, opened a competing brewery in Dayton. He ran his City Brewery with partners Hohlberg, Schmidt, Godde, and Julius G. Mary until 1887.

DOUGLAS

Frank Thompson opened a small brewery at Douglas in 1890, but closed it by the end of the year.

ELLENSBURG

Theodore Heft built the City Brewery in Ellensburg, then known as East Kittitas, in 1880 on Anderson Street. M. Dewiscourt acquired the brewery in 1887 and ran it with partners Hoscheid and Shuller until 1900. The brewery was dormant for about three years, then in 1904 it was reopened at Second and Sampson Streets by George Taylor.

In 1908 Taylor sold the City Brewery to Adolph Krulish, who owned it until 1911. In that year Frederick E. Broese bought the plant and with a partner named Richter brewed lager beer at 505 East Second Street until 1916.

Another brewery was opened in Ellensburg by the St. Louis Brewing Co. in 1895. The location was 414 West Fifth Street. St. Louis Brewing sold the plant in 1906 to new owners who did business under the name Ellensburg Brewing & Malting Co. They operated the brewery until state prohibition closed all breweries in 1916.

After Repeal the brewery was reactivated as Ellensburg Brewing Co., Inc. and was in business from 1934 to 1937. Another name change to Mutual Brewing Co., Inc. came about in 1937, and the company continued until finally closing in 1943.

In 1884 John Blomquist, a Swedish brewer and rancher, owned a brewery in Ellensburg, which he kept for four years.

Also, Chang and Becker had a short-lived brewery in town from 1885 to 1887, and James Dickson had a small operation from 1886 to 1888.

EVERETT

There were two breweries in Everett, each lasting just a few years. The Washington Brewing Company maintained a local brewery from 1899 to 1904, and the Everett Brewing Company, at 33rd and Smith Avenue, brewed from 1904 until 1916 with Albert Burke as manager.

FAIRHAVEN

Fairhaven was a pioneer town (now part of the city of Bellingham) located on Bellingham Bay, encompassing the southerly portion

The Everett Brewing Company used this wagon for its deliveries in 1905. The photo shows part of the brewery's saloon.

of the populated area on the bay. Richard Asbeck operated a small brewery at Fairhaven from 1888 to 1891.

FARMINGTON

Andrew Christ had a brewery in this Whitman County community from 1884 to 1893.

GRANITE FALLS

In 1893 Henry Kern attempted to open a brewery in Granite Falls, Snohomish County, but there is no record of beer production. He closed the same year.

KALAMA

John Schauble ran a brewery here from 1874 to 1880. In 1878 he sold 105 barrels of beer.

Kalama is presently the home of the Hart Brewing Co. (See Chapter Six.)

LA CAMAS

La Camas was a small settlement in Lewis County, about three miles east of present Onalaska. The community's 500 people were centered about a lumber mill, a paper mill, and a flour mill. John Nager had a small brewery at La Camas from 1885 until 1888.

LOOMIS

Charles Langendorf, with partners Anderson and Garrett, had a brewery in this Okanogan community from 1900 to 1904. They sold the brewery to Frank Lintz, who ran it until 1916.

MEDICAL LAKE

In 1882 Thomas Robinette and George E. Staples each tried to start a brewery in Medical Lake, but they were both out of business by the next year.

MILES

The Fort Spokane Brewery, located on the road to the army post of that name near Miles, was established by Bernard Bockemuehl in 1887. Bockemuehl was a German brewer who had worked in Milwaukee breweries before coming west, and he found a ready market for his lager at nearby Fort Spokane. Until the post was

By 1890 the Fort Spokane Brewery near Miles was supplying the nearby army post with 2,000 barrels of beer annually.

decommissioned in 1898, the happy brewer supplied 2,000 barrels of beer a year to the thirsty soldiers.

There is a story told that Bockemuehl's black horse, Coaley, was so trained to deliver wagonloads of beer kegs to the fort that he would make the trip alone, driverless. When the kegs had been unloaded, Coaley would trot straight back to the brewery.

The Fort Spokane Brewery operated until 1906.

MUKILTEO

George Cantrini began a brewery here in 1878. The first year George sold 240 barrels of beer, and in 1879 he sold 432. In 1882 S. N. Snyder acquired the brewery and ran it until 1884.

NORTHPORT

The Northport Brewing Company was in business in this northeastern Washington town from 1897 until 1905, supplying local bottled and keg lager and ice.

OCOSTA

There was a small brewery in the promising new railroad town of Ocosta-by-the-Sea, as it was then called, built in 1892 by Richard Sandbach. Unfortunately, railroad changes and a financial panic in 1893 sent the townspeople packing, and by the next year Ocosta was almost a ghost town—and the brewery was empty.

OLYMPIA

In addition to the famous Olympia Brewing Company (see Chapter Five), there were two other breweries in Olympia, both of which predated Olympia Brewing, but they were lost in the shadow of the Tumwater giant. Brothers J. C. and J. R. Wood owned the Pacific Brewery in downtown Olympia from 1874 to 1880. In 1879 they sold 264 barrels of beer. And Xavier Hosneder had the Bohemia Brewery, at the north edge of town, from 1880 until 1888.

OROVILLE

In 1905, Fritz Grathwohl, a brewer from Bellingham, and his partner E. J. Strelau built the Oroville Brewing Company. With an excellent business location on the main road through the Okanogan country to Canada, the brewery was immediately popular. Selling ice to saloons, hotels, restaurants, and homes was a lucrative side business for Fritz. Blocks of pure ice were cut during the winter from Blue and Wannacut Lakes and kept through the summer in the brewery's immense insulated wooden icehouse.

Fritz Grathwohl was a rotund, happy brewer who took pleasure in participating in and contributing money and beer to civic and regional functions. He loved parades and rode in them at every opportunity up on the high seat of his bunting-draped beer wagon. Heinrich, the *Bierhund* (beer dog), rode on the seat with Fritz. Fritz had brought Heinrich with him from Bellingham and the two were inseparable. Little Heinrich, happy and rotund like Fritz, was very fond of his master's product. Spending nearly all his waking and sleeping hours close to the vats and casks where he could beg frequent saucers of lager, Heinrich was a contented *Bierhund.* Fritz Grathwohl claimed that Heinrich had an excellent

The Koller Brewery in Orting, some years after it closed in 1898.

sense of beer quality and would lap up no lager but the one brewed at the Oroville Brewing Company.

The brewery operated until closed by prohibition in 1916.

ORTING

G. Koller & Co. had a brewery in this Pierce County community from 1891 until 1898.

PALOUSE

A brewery and saloon were built in Palouse City by Sam Dimmick and partners Choate and Pelkes in 1882. The Palouse Brewery, on the south side of Main Street, was the only building east of Bridge Street that survived a devastating fire on May 7, 1888. The brewery was by the river, but the story goes that it was saved by blankets soaked in beer that were spread on the roof and down the walls.

John Schmidt bought the brewery in 1888; he sold it to his partner Saunders in 1898. Saunders and McGraw had the brewery until 1901, when Charles V. Drazan purchased the plant and changed the name from Palouse Brewery to the Palouse Brewing Company. The brewery stayed in business until 1916.

PASCO

A company known as Northern Pacific Brewing and Malting Co. was formed in 1890. That same year the name was changed to Milwaukee Brewing and Ice Mfg. Co. It was licensed until 1892, although local historians and Franklin County Historical Society records have no further information on the brewery.

PATAHA

A small brewery was built in 1882 at Pataha City, near Pomeroy in Garfield County. Jacob Bihlmaier was the brewmaster. He learned his trade in Germany and operated the City Brewery with his partner E. J. Wolf until 1890. Thomas W. Shannon then acquired the brewery and closed it two years later.

POMEROY

The Scholl brothers, Ernst and Emil, built one of Pomeroy's earliest businesses. Their Columbia Brewery was established in 1878.

Ernst and Emil Scholl were born in Hamburg, Germany, and

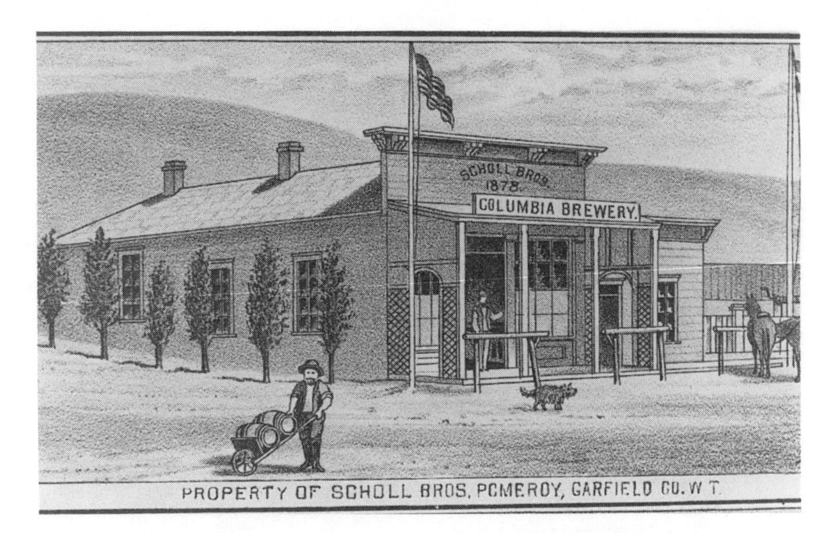

The Columbia Brewery, built by Emil and Ernst Scholl in Pomeroy, was the third American brewery operated by the brothers. They made beer there from 1878 to 1892.

both left for a life at sea when still in their teens. After some years as a sailor, Ernst came to America to live in 1850, followed a few years later by brother Emil. They worked at John Stahl's brewery in Canyon City, Oregon and went with him to Walla Walla, where they helped at his brewery there.

In 1884 the Scholls sold the Columbia Brewery to John Rehorn, who ran it until 1892.

A competing brewery opened for a short time in 1889. It was called the Garfield Brewery and it closed within two years.

PORT ANGELES

In 1902 Charles Hirsch and Fred Jensen built the Port Angeles Brewing Co. at Third and Tumwater Streets, at the mouth of Tumwater Creek. Two years later they changed the name of the brewery to Angeles Brewing and Malting Co. A brewer from Pittsburgh, Adolph Oettinger, was brewmaster at the Hirsch and Jensen brewery from 1902 until 1907.

The brewery produced 6,000 barrels of "Angeles Beer" annually, most of which was sold in the Seattle area. For a time, the

This 1903 view of the Angeles Brewing and Malting Company in Port Angeles shows the brewery at its peak.

An example of a humorous advertising design for "Angeles Beer," circa 1905.

brewery ran its own freight ship, the *Albion,* between Port Angeles and Seattle.

In 1914 J.F. Janeke was brewery manager. The brewery was closed by state prohibition in 1916.

PORT ORCHARD

The brewery in Port Orchard began as the Kitsap Brewing Company. It was built at 1209 Bay Street in 1934. The next year the name was changed to one more familiar to longtime Washington beer lovers, Silver Springs Brewing Co. Silver Springs brewed "DeLuxe Beer" and "Old Style" beer in bottles and cans. At one time, the six-story brewery was the tallest building in Kitsap County.

One of Washington's most popular post-Prohibition breweries, the Silver Springs Brewing Co. in Port Orchard, brewed "Old Style" and "DeLuxe" beer in bottles and cans.

The brewery was sold to the Columbia (Heidelberg) Brewing Co. of Tacoma in 1941, and was closed in 1950.

PORT TOWNSEND

There were two breweries in picturesque Port Townsend. The first was built by William Goelert in 1874 on Water Street. He sold the brewery in 1877 to William Roesch, who ran it for two years, selling in 1879 to Charles Eisenbeis. Roesch then moved to Oregon, where he had breweries in Heppner and Pendleton.

Charles Eisenbeis was a leading Port Townsend citizen by the time he bought the brewery in 1879. Born in Germany, he first arrived in Port Townsend in 1858 and opened a bakery. In 1861 Charles moved to Steilacoom and was a partner in the Martin Schmeig brewery there. The partnership was ended in April 1864, and the dissolution agreement read: "It was agreed that Eisenbeis shall not, for the term of 15 years after, engage in the manufacture of Lager Beer & Ale within the District of Puget Sound nor shall any of his agents or partners in business."

Evidently Charles had learned some terrific brewing secrets and recipes while with Schmeig, and Martin did not want competition from Eisenbeis when he left. In any event, Charles kept to the agreement, for he did not enter into the brewing business until he bought the Port Townsend Brewery fifteen years later.

Charles Eisenbeis was also one of the primary builders in town, constructing or having an interest in two banks, a hotel, a short-line railroad, a steel and nail works, a brickyard, and a real estate business. He also built a large, castle-like residence that still stands today.

Eisenbeis operated the brewery for nine years, closing it in 1888.

Port Townsend's second brewery was built in 1906 at Monroe and Washington Streets. The Port Townsend Brewing Co. was owned by German brewer J. Duttenhoefer. He brewed "Townsend" lager beer in kegs and bottles until selling the brewery in 1909 to Leopold Schmidt of the Olympia Brewing Co. in Tumwater. The Schmidt interests continued brewing "Townsend Beer" until closed by the dark days of state prohibition in 1916.

The Port Townsend Brewing Co. was built in 1906.

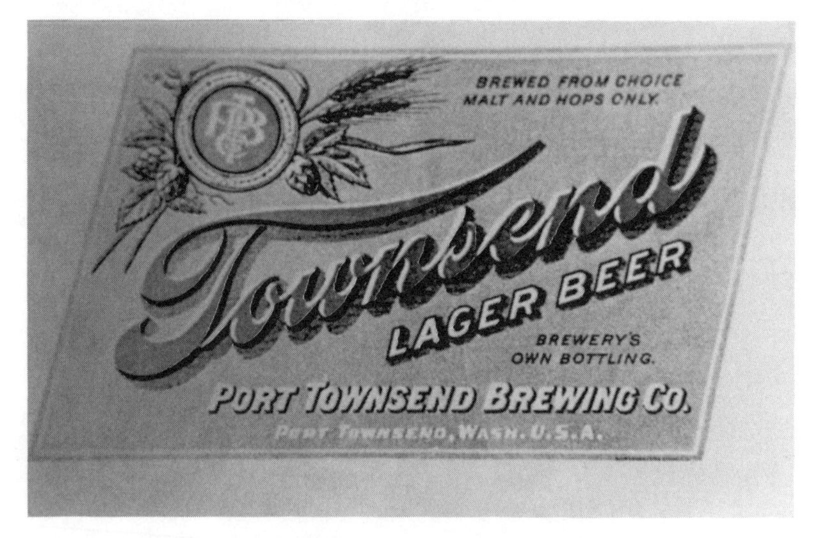

"Townsend Lager Beer" was made in Port Townsend from 1906 until 1916.

REPUBLIC

Joseph Winkler built the Republic Brewing and Malting Co. in 1898 near a good spring 2½ miles east of town. His business partner was George Falligan, who managed the finances and marketing while Joseph tended the brewery.

Brewmaster Winkler was born in St. Paul, Minnesota of a German brewer father. Joseph learned the trade at an early age and worked at breweries in St. Paul and Montana. He met George Falligan in Butte, and together they moved west to Republic to open a brewery.

In 1904 a third partner, Arnold Maschka, joined the firm and for some years had charge of the brewery saloon, located in another part of town. Maschka bought out the other partners' interests in 1913 and ran the brewery alone until 1916.

ROSLYN

The brewery in Roslyn was built in 1890 by William Dewitt and Frank Groger. In 1892 Rachor and Duerrwachter acquired the plant, and in 1893 A. F. Kuhl and the Schlotfeldt brothers bought out Rachor and continued to operate the brewery with Ernest and Charles Duerrwachter. It was called the Roslyn Brewing Company.

The brewery was leased to the Schlotfeldt brothers from 1896 to 1901. Kuhl took control again in 1901 and ran the brewery until 1913.

RUBY

There was a small short-term brewery in this Pend Oreille County community from 1888 to 1893. It was built by L. Rachenberger, and sold to John Wise in 1891. The brewery doors closed in 1893.

SEATTLE

Seattle, like Portland, had a plethora of breweries from the 1870s until state prohibition. The undisputed monarch among these Puget Sound beer makers was Andrew Hemrich and his Seattle Brewing & Malting Company (now Rainier). Over a period of time, particularly with a great consolidation effort in the 1890s, Andrew and his brothers, Alvin and Louis, brought most of the other breweries into the "House of Hemrich." (The Rainier saga is told in Chapter Five.)

Washington Brewery. The first brewery in Seattle was the Washington Brewery, owned by A. B. Rabbeson & Co. The exact date of its establishment is not known. It was operating by the spring of 1864, however, because at that time Rabbeson was advertising that his brewery was making beer, porter, and cream ale.

In 1865 the Washington Brewery was owned by McLoon and Sherman, and was located at Fourth Avenue and Yesler Way. Stuart Crichton acquired the brewery in 1872 and renamed it the Seattle Brewery. Several years later, Andrew Slorah and his partner King bought the brewery. Soon King retired and Slorah ran the brewery alone for a few years. In 1878 the Slorah brewery sold 1,652 barrels of beer.

Ernest Romey purchased the plant in 1884, and by the end of 1888 it was dismantled.

North Pacific Brewery. Martin Schmeig, an early Northwest brewer from Steilacoom, opened a brewery with Joseph Butterfield in 1865 on the southwest corner of First Avenue and Columbia Street. Butterfield soon left the firm; the brewery was then owned by Schmeig and a new partner, Brown.

Martin Schmeig lost his wife in 1877 and decided to return to

Martin Schmeig opened his North Pacific Brewery in Seattle on the southwest corner of First and Columbia in 1865. It was Seattle's second brewery.

Germany. He left his North Pacific Brewery in the charge of August Mehlhorn, and later that year sold the brewery to him.

August Mehlhorn was trained as a bricklayer and weaver in the Old Country, but he gained brewery experience after crossing the Atlantic to America in 1867. He began working at Schmeig's North Pacific Brewery in 1875 as a driver on a beer wagon. He was a fast learner and quickly rose to administrative jobs. After he acquired the brewery from Martin Schmeig, Mehlhorn brewed "Mehlhorn" beer with great success for eight years.

In 1885 August Mehlhorn dismantled the North Pacific Brewery equipment and buildings. He sold the equipment to Andrew Slorah, who constructed a new building on the east side of Lincoln Street, between Fifth and Sixth Avenues, near Lake Union. Continuing the name North Pacific Brewery, he operated the new plant for several years.

Slorah sold the brewery in 1888 and retired to an easygoing life as a saloonkeeper. Julius Weigert, the new North Pacific owner, ran the brewery until 1891; then he sold it and went into the saloon business too, at his Brewery Saloon on Yesler and the Log Cabin Saloon on Columbia.

Charles A. Saake, a brewer and cooper, bought the North Pacific Brewery and held it until 1897, when he sold out to Hemrich interests and moved north to Skagway, Alaska to build another brewery.

The Hemrichs moved the brewery to Howard (now Yale) Avenue at Republican Street and operated it as part of their empire until 1916.

Cantierri Brewery. George Cantierri had a tiny lager brewery in 1874 to supply his saloon and a few other customers. He closed at the end of 1875.

Claussen-Sweeney Brewing Co. In 1884 Edward F. Sweeney and W. J. Rule built a large brewery in what was then Georgetown (the present industrial area in south Seattle, just north of Boeing Field). Sweeney was one of the few non-German brewers in the Northwest.

Rule sold his interest, and in 1888 Sweeney reorganized the company with a German brewmaster, Hans J. Claussen from Schleswig-Holstein in northern Germany. After arriving in the

The Claussen-Sweeney Brewery in Seattle had a capacity of one million gallons of beer in 1893.

The caption on this 1893 photo reads:
"Raising glasses of Claussen Beer in the Union Saloon."

United States, Herr Claussen worked at the Fredericksburg Brewery in San Jose, California and at the National Brewing Company in San Francisco.

The Claussen-Sweeney Brewery grew to an immense size, and in 1893 had a 1,000,000-gallon capacity. By the end of 1893 Claussen-Sweeney had merged with the Hemrich empire, which by then was known as the Seattle Brewing & Malting Company, forerunner of Rainier.

In 1901 Hans Claussen formed a stock company and built another brewery in south Seattle. The brewery remained in business until 1916.

Albert Braun Brewing Association. Albert Braun formed a company with several financial contributors in 1890. He brewed "Columbia Beer" for three years at the south Seattle location before merging with Hemrich's Seattle Brewing & Malting Co. in 1893. Seattle Brewing & Malting was organized in 1892–93 to consolidate the Braun Brewery, Claussen-Sweeney, and several Hemrich Brothers Brewing Co. plants. (The story is told in the Rainier section of Chapter Five.)

Julius Weigert Brewing Co. In 1889 Julius Weigert had a modest brewery on Lake Union. He produced porter and ale, but the brewery closed at the end of 1890.

West & Co. Brewery. J. H. West built a small ale and porter brewery in 1899 at Westlake Avenue and Galer Street, near Lake Union. He sold the plant the next year to W. H. Armstrong. The brewery had two successive name changes, Seattle Ale and Porter Co. and American Brewing Co. It went out of business in 1903.

Standard Brewing Co. This brewery was built in 1901 at 3255 21st Avenue West. Later that year it was purchased by the Claussen Brewing Association and soon came into the Hemrich empire.

Spellmire-West Brewing Co. In 1905 brothers G. H. and E. D. Spellmire, together with J. H. West, established the Spellmire-West Brewery at 1320 Almy Street. The partners changed the name to Washington Brewing Company in 1913 and continued to operate their brewery until Prohibition in 1916.

Independent Brewing Co. Partners Loeb and Moyses built a brewery in 1902 at Eighth Avenue South and Pacific in south Seattle. In the shadow of the Hemrich breweries, but never a part of them, Loeb and Moyses chose an apt name—Independent Brewing Co. The brewery closed in 1916.

Apex Brewing Co. Apex Brewing Co. was a Hemrich company, at Ninth Avenue South (now Airport Way South) and Hanford, which ran from 1933 to 1937. It marketed "Apex Beer" in cans and bottles. This plant originally was the historic Bay View Brewery. (See Rainier story, Chapter Five.)

Horluck Brewing Co. George F. Horluck built his brewery in 1934 at 606/610 Westlake Avenue at Mercer. The brand name, remembered by many Seattle beer drinkers, was "Horluck's."

The Horluck brewery was absorbed by Seattle Brewing and Malting in 1939, owned at that time by Emil and Fritz Sick. In 1944 the plant was doing business as Sicks' Century Brewery. The brewery closed in 1957, and the equipment and personnel were merged into the immense Sicks' Rainier Brewing Co.

Pilsener Brewing Co., Inc. In 1934 the Pilsener Brewing Co. was opened at 548 First Avenue South. Plagued by financial difficulties, they closed the next year.

Western Brewing Co. This brewery at 5225 East Marginal Way was a branch plant of the mighty Hemrich empire from 1934 until the end of 1940.

Elmer E. Hemrich Brewery Co. Elmer Hemrich, nephew of

Seattle brewing magnate Andrew Hemrich, was born in 1890. Through his youth and early adult years Elmer worked in the Hemrich breweries in various capacities, including managing the Aberdeen Brewery.

Immediately following Repeal, Elmer purchased the old Columbia Breweries, Inc. plant in Tacoma and brewed beer there for two years.

In October 1935 Elmer sold his interest in Columbia Breweries and returned to Seattle, where he established a modest brewery under his own name. He soon changed it to Gold Seal Breweries, Inc. "Gold Seal" beer had a following in the Northwest until 1940.

SELAH

Selah's Yakima Valley Brewing Company was established in 1938. It was located on Railroad Avenue next to the present Tree Top Corporation. "Selah Springs" beer was popular in central Washington but did not find a wide distribution outside the area.

Eventually Fred Martin bought the brewery and sold lager under his "Martin's Beer" label in old cone-top cans and bottles. The brewery closed in 1954.

SNOHOMISH

A brewery was started at Snohomish in 1890 by two distinctly German fellows, Zweifelhofer and Wohlgethan. In 1891 Herr Zweifelhofer had a new partner, Jehli, and the next year Carl C. Wagner bought the brewery. It was a short-lived beer-making plant, closing in 1893.

SPOKANE

Spokane has hosted many breweries over the years, all of them now gone, except for two recent microbreweries that carry on the tradition.

Peterson Brewery. The first beermaker in Spokane Falls was M. Peterson & Co. in 1879. The Peterson Brewery went through a succession of owners—L. Weisgerber, Amelia Berry, R. E. A. Mueller, and Koehler—until it was finally closed in 1891.

Palmtag & Wilson Brewery. Palmtag and Wilson operated a brewery in Spokane Falls from 1884 to 1887.

Hencoe Brewery. Theodore and Charles Hencoe established their Hencoe Brewery at Fifth Avenue and Ash Street in 1886.

Theodore Hencoe, the older brother, was one of those old-time Pacific Northwest brewers who learned the trade early in life, apprenticing in the brewery business in Offenburg, Germany at age fourteen. At twenty-three he came to America, where he worked for large breweries in St. Louis and San Francisco.

In 1886 Theodore and brother Charles arrived at the bustling trade center on the Spokane River and erected the Hencoe Brewery. The brothers made beer in Spokane until 1899, when they sold the brewery to Reinhard Martin.

Like Theodore Hencoe, Reinhard Martin was a master brewer who learned the trade as a youth in Germany. Reinhard arrived in New York in 1883 and worked in a brewery there for six years. In 1889 he came to Spokane and was a foreman at the New York Brewery for three years. He worked for the Galland-Burke Brewery for another three years, and in 1895 moved to Missoula, Montana, where he built his own brewery.

Reinhard returned to Spokane in 1899 and purchased the Hencoes' plant, which he continued to call the Hencoe Brewery. When Martin took over, the brewery had a beer-making capacity of 15,000 barrels per year, although sales were actually much less.

This is an 1890 view of the New York Brewery in Spokane.
It stood on the northeast corner of Front and Washington Streets.

New York Brewery workers pose in front of the brewery in 1895.

The brewery was acquired by the Spokane Brewing and Malting Company in 1901 and continued under the Hencoe Brewery name until 1916.

Gorkow's New York Brewery. Rudolph Gorkow built a massive three-story brick and stone brewery in 1886 at the corner of Front Avenue and Washington Street. It employed about twenty men year-round and made a popular lager known as "New York Beer."

Rudolph Gorkow died in 1896, and his estate operated the brewery until 1900, when it was acquired by the Spokane Brewing and Malting Company. The brewery closed in 1904.

Union Brewery & Malthouse. John G. Hieber established his Union Brewery at Twelfth Avenue and Spruce Street in 1890. He sold the brewery to Charles Theis fifteen years later in 1905. Theis moved the equipment and men into a larger building on Second Avenue, between Cedar and Walnut, and called it Inland Brewing and Malting Company. He brewed beer at that location for ten years.

Following Repeal in 1933, the old brewery was modernized and reopened by Bohemian Breweries, Inc., a branch of the Atlantic Brewing Co. of Chicago. Bohemian Breweries brewed the popular "Bohemian Club Beer" until closing its doors in 1962.

After Prohibition, the old Inland Brewing & Malting Co. was reopened by Bohemian Breweries, Inc. "Bohemian Club Beer" was famous in the Northwest until the brewery closed in 1962. (Photo circa 1952.)

Richter Brewery. George Richter started a small brewery in 1891, but by the end of the next year it was closed.

Galland-Burke Brewing and Malting Co. In 1860 Julius Galland was born in Oregon to German parents. His early business life included partnership with his brothers Theodore, Adolph, and Samuel in the mercantile business. They owned stores in Oregon and San Francisco. In 1883 the brothers Galland moved to Washington, where they ran general stores in Palouse and Farmington.

The brewery business had always appealed to the Gallands, since it had been a family tradition in the Old Country. So in 1891 the Galland brothers and a partner named Burke constructed the Galland-Burke Brewery in Spokane. The immense structure was located on Broadway Avenue, between Post and Lincoln Streets, overlooking the namesake falls of the city. Julius was president of the company, and the other brothers were officers.

Galland-Burke beer was marketed throughout Washington and in Oregon, Idaho, Montana, and British Columbia.

In 1902 the plant was sold to the Spokane Brewing and Malting Company and continued until 1916. After Prohibition the

In 1938 the Spokane Breweries plant sat on the old 1891 Galland-Burke site.

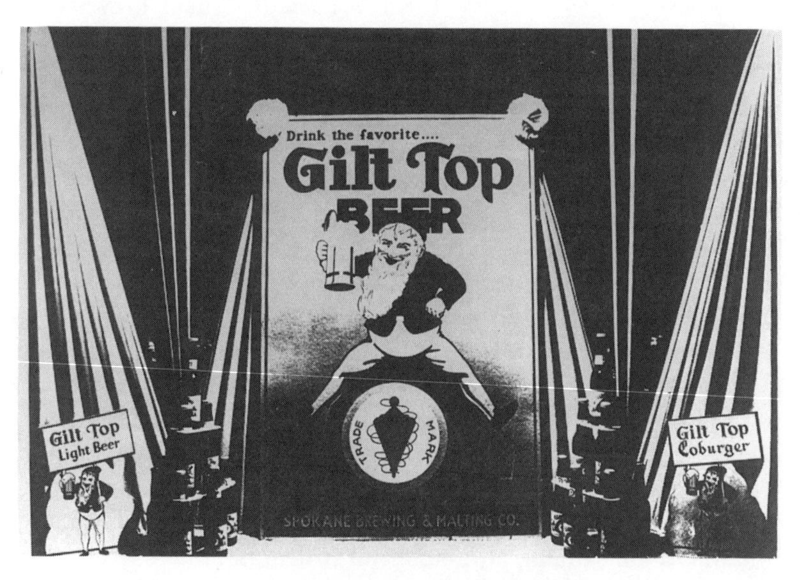

"Gilt Top Beer" was the pride of Spokane Brewing & Malting. Photo circa 1937.

brew plant was reactivated in 1934 and made "Gilt Top Beer" until 1940, at which time the brewery name was changed to The Spokane Brewery, Inc.

The business was sold to Emil Sick of Rainier Brewing Co. in 1944, and it was used as a branch brewery of the Rainier Company from 1958 until 1962.

American Brewing Co. A small brewery under this name was established in 1902 at 1124 East Sprague Avenue. It closed in 1904.

B. Schade Brewing Co. The Barnhardt Schade brewery was built in 1904 on the northeast corner of Sheridan and Front Streets. It closed in 1916 and reopened in 1934 as the Golden Age Breweries, Inc. The "Golden Age" beer label was well-known and popular in the Pacific Northwest until 1948. In that year the brewery was sold to the Bohemian Company and operated as Bohemian Breweries, Inc., Plant #2 until it closed in 1950.

Panhandle Brewing Co. In 1913 the Panhandle Brewing Co. opened its doors at 124 Pacific Avenue, but stayed in business only until 1915. Panhandle Brewing also had a brewery in Coeur d'Alene, Idaho at the same time.

Office of Paul G. Schade at the Schade Brewing Company on Trent Avenue in Spokane. Photo circa 1909.

Goetz Breweries, Inc. The Goetz Brewery was founded at 1107 North Pearl Street in 1934. Three years later it was acquired by Spokane Breweries, Inc., and the next year the Pearl Street plant was closed. Spokane Breweries continued to make "Goetz Beer" in the main brewery at Broadway and Lincoln.

SPRAGUE

R. O. Porak was a brewer from Germany. In 1881 he started a brewery in Sprague, the foundation of which can still be seen in the northeast part of town. This Old Country brewer had previously purchased a brewery in The Dalles, Oregon in 1878, which he continued to own for a few years after moving to Sprague. Porak's Sprague Brewery used local barley and had hops shipped in from the Puyallup Valley.

Bräumeister Porak had all the business he could handle supplying the town's thirteen saloons in the 1880s, as well as neighboring communities. He brought in partners over the years and for a time the brewery was known as Porak & Desserts Brewery, and later, Porak and Moerder.

On August 3, 1895, a fire wiped out most of Sprague's business buildings, taking Porak's brewery and residence. He soon rebuilt on the same spot.

The Sprague Pioneer Picnic Association held annual three-day celebrations at the fairgrounds, and during these socials R. O. Porak's beer flowed free—literally. Though he was a sound businessman most of the year, R. O. always said he was honored to provide barrels of his finest lager for the annual town picnic to show his appreciation for Sprague's support over the years.

As a lucrative side business, the brewer contracted with the Northern Pacific Railroad to ship ice, cut during the winter from nearby Colville (now Sprague) Lake, to consumers in other parts of Washington.

The Sprague brewery closed in 1906.

STEILACOOM

The manufacture of beer was among the earliest industrial activities in Washington, and the first brewery north of the Columbia River was Nicholas Delin's little 1854 brewhouse in what was then known as the Steilacoom District. To be more precise, the brewery was probably at or near the site of Delin's sawmill on the southwest shore of Commencement Bay, where Tacoma stands today. The records, however, show only that Nicholas had a brewery in the Steilacoom District.

In any event, the Delin Brewery lasted only a short time; by 1857 Nicholas had moved to Seattle where he worked in building construction.

Martin Schmeig established a brewery in the town of Steilacoom in 1860 with partner Joseph Butterfield. The firm name was Schmeig's Brewery. In December 1861 Schmeig and Charles Eisenbeis formed a partnership, Schmeig & Eisenbeis, manufacturing lager beer, ale, and porter. The partnership dissolved in April 1864. It was agreed that Eisenbeis would not engage in beer-making for fifteen years in the Puget Sound country. Charles kept the agreement, purchasing a brewery in Port Townsend fifteen years later.

The next year, 1865, Martin Schmeig sold the brewery to John Lukenbein and moved to Seattle, where he opened another brewery with his former partner, Joseph Butterfield.

Meanwhile, Lukenbein ran the Steilacoom brewery with a man named Anton Mueller until 1878, when they leased the property

The Schafer & Howard Brewery in Steilacoom was taken over in 1889 by the Northern Pacific Railroad.

to John Flammer. He brewed for five years under the banner of Puget Sound Brewery, then returned control to Lukenbein.

Next in line to operate the little brewery was Ignatz Furst and his partner Joseph Baumeister, who leased it in 1879 and kept the name Puget Sound Brewery. Two years later, Lukenbein leased the plant to Gollfried Gamble and Meyer Kaufman.

John Lukenbein died in 1887, and the property came back to his estate. In 1890 the brewery was sold to Henry Rupp, who ran it for a short time.

Another brewery in Steilacoom was established on Starling Street in 1873 by Wolf Schaefer. He had an early partner named Zoberst, but by 1878 his only partner was Dennis K. Howard. In that year the Schaefer & Howard Brewery, as it was then called, brewed 1,810 barrels of beer. Schaefer died in 1889, and the brewery was acquired by the Northern Pacific Railroad. The company closed the brewery in 1891.

TACOMA

Donau Brewing Co. The first brewery in Tacoma was the Donau Brewing Co., established in 1884 by former Steilacoom brewer Ignatz Furst. When the tower of the Donau Brewery was blown down in a ferocious windstorm in November 1889, brewmaster Furst announced that the vats were undamaged and plenty of beer would be available to help Tacoma celebrate Washington's new statehood on November 11th.

The Donau Brewery was sold to Anton Huth's Pacific Brewing and Malting Co. in 1899. Huth closed the Donau in 1903.

Stegmann Brewery. In the same year the Donau Brewery was established, a German brewer named Diedrich Stegmann opened a modest brewery in Tacoma. He soon had a partner, Lusthoff, and together they brewed a lager for the local trade until 1888. In that year the brewery was sold to Portland brewer George Herrall, who used it as a Washington branch of his United States Brewing Co.

Four years later, in 1891, Herrall sold the Tacoma branch brewery to new owners. It was called the Milwaukee Brewing Co. and was located at 23rd and Jefferson, just two blocks from Anton Huth's burgeoning Pacific Brewing and Malting Company. Huth purchased the plant, renaming it Pacific Brewing and Malting–Milwaukee Branch Brewery. In 1899 the Milwaukee Branch was merged into the main brewery, which by then covered fifty lots.

Neitzel Brewery. In late 1884 Frederick Neitzel opened a tiny brewery to supply his saloon and a number of other local customers with a special-recipe lager that was reportedly quite tasty. Three years later, before Neitzel could complete his brewery expansion plans, he was shot and killed in his saloon by a robber on the day before Christmas Eve. Hufeisen and Horning acquired the Neitzel Brewery & Saloon, but by 1890 they were closed.

Pacific Brewing & Malting Co. In 1888 young John D. Scholl, proprietor of a small but successful brewery known as the New Tacoma Brewery, decided to expand. He had been turning out 900 barrels of beer annually, but the ambitious brewer wanted to build a major plant, one that could brew a hundred times that amount.

Fortunately, in that year John Scholl met Herr Anton Huth, a well-to-do master brewer of some note, trained in the Old Country, who was looking for a brewing partner in Tacoma. They formed a partnership and began a brewing tradition that was to last for nearly thirty years.

Anton Huth was born in Darmstadt, near Frankfurt, Germany in 1854. There Anton learned the trade of brewer and maltster, obtaining both a technical and practical knowledge of the business at the heart of the beer-making industry.

In the fall of 1872, shortly after his father died, young Huth came to America with his mother. Though only eighteen years old, Anton got a good brewery job in Louisville, Kentucky, where he worked for fourteen years.

In 1885 Anton moved west to Portland, where he became a foreman at Henry Weinhard's brewery. Two years later he relocated across the Columbia River and bought a minor interest in Anton Young's Star Brewery. The next year, 1888, Huth moved north to Tacoma to build his own brewery. There he met John Scholl.

The Huth-Scholl enterprise was known as the Puget Sound Brewery. They had been in business for only three years, however, when Anton bought out Scholl's interest. Six years later, in 1897, Huth reorganized with a new partner named William Virges and incorporated the business as Pacific Brewing and Malting Company.

Huth and Virges enlarged their brewery, and in the process purchased total interest in the Donau Brewery and the nearby

In 1909 the Pacific Brewing Company was the second largest in Washington, covering fifty lots with thirteen buildings.

Milwaukee Brewery. By 1909 Pacific Brewing and Malting Company was the second largest brewing concern in Washington, surpassed only by Seattle Brewing & Malting—now Rainier. In the first decade of this century, Pacific Brewing's thirteen large structures on South 25th Street, between C Street and Jefferson, occupied fifty lots, and the brewery was producing 200,000 barrels of beer per year. Its "Pacific" and "Tacoma" labels were popular throughout the West, and the brewery boasted customers around the world.

The glory of Pacific Brewing lasted only until Washington's state prohibition became effective in January 1916. Nine months later, in September, Anton Huth passed away.

After the old brewer's death, William Virges, who had been the secretary and treasurer of the company, took over as president. But it was an empty empire, and Virges was a king with no realm. The ghostly brewery buildings stood idle for three years until Virges settled for using them as a soap and oil factory in 1919. His National Soap Co. was successful with a worldwide market for its chief product, Playmate Soap.

The Pacific Brewing and Malting Co. buildings have had a

long history: first as a brewery, then a soap company, a chemical factory, and an ice manufacturer. The remaining structures at 25th and Jefferson are still used today by storage firms and other businesses.

The old brick brewery was placed on the National Register of Historic Places in 1978.

Columbia Brewing Co. In 1900 a German brewer named Emil Kleise established the Columbia Brewing Co. on South C Street, not far from the giant Pacific Brewing and Malting Company. Though much smaller than his nearby competitor at first, Kleise's brewery lasted for 79 years and became one of the largest on the Pacific Coast.

While records of the early days of Columbia Brewery are scarce, it is known that Emil Kleise was owner, president, and brewmaster of his plant until statewide prohibition in 1916. He died the next year. One of the original brands at Columbia Brewery was a name that would become famous after Prohibition, "Alt Heidelberg."

During the Prohibition years, Columbia Brewery was able to stay in business by manufacturing soft drinks. Among the nonalcoholic products were "Birch Beer," described as being akin to

EVERYBODY KNOWS

IT'S BETTER

ON DRAUGHT IN BOTTLES
IN KEGLINED CANS

The clear, sparkling goodness of Alt Heidelberg Makes it a favorite no matter how you enjoy it.

COLUMBIA BREWERIES, Inc.

Tacoma—Offices in principal Northwestern Cities

Columbia Breweries ad of the 1930s.

From 1900 to 1949 the Heidelberg plant was known as Columbia Breweries, Inc. This photo of the abandoned brewery was taken at 2120 South C Street, Tacoma, in 1987.

root beer but with a birch-bark flavor; "Chocolate Soldier"; "Blue Jay," a grape drink; and "Green River." The plant also produced a beverage called "Alt Heidelberg Ginger Ale."

Recognizing the possibility of Repeal 7½ months before it actually occurred, Elmer Hemrich, of the Hemrich brothers' Seattle brewing empire, bought the Columbia Brewery. It was enlarged, modernized, and reorganized as Columbia Breweries, Inc., and Hemrich served as president from 1933 to 1935, when he sold his interest.

Joseph Lancer became president of the brewery in 1935, succeeded four years later by Norman Davis. Two popular labels at

Columbia at that time were "Alt Heidelberg" and "Alt Pilsener Lager Beer."

In 1941 Columbia purchased the Silver Springs Brewery in Port Orchard, where "Hartz Western Style" beer, as well as other brands, continued to be produced under the Silver Springs label. The Port Orchard brewery was closed in 1950 and the Silver Springs label transferred to another brewery acquired by Columbia. (See Northwest Brewing Co.)

The name was changed to Heidelberg Brewing Co. in 1949 during Davis's time as head of the company. Nine years later, in 1958, the old brewery came under new ownership when it was acquired by Carling Brewing Company of Canada, although it was still called the Heidelberg Brewery. In November 1974 Carling and National Brewing Co., also a Canadian firm, merged to form the Carling-National Breweries, Inc., and the Tacoma plant became officially the Heidelberg division of Carling-National.

Three deep artesian wells, pumping 66,000 gallons, provided water for such national favorites as "Heidelberg," "Tuborg Gold," "Black Label," "Columbia," and "Colt 45 Malt Liquor."

The historic brewery established by Emil Kleise in 1900 was acquired by the G. Heileman Brewing Co. of La Crosse, Wisconsin, and closed its doors in 1979 after three-quarters of a century of brewing. The buildings stood idle as the equipment was slowly disposed of; the last remnants were sold at auction in 1986.

Kopp Brewery. Christopher Kopp attempted to start a small brewery in Tacoma in 1904, but by the next year he was closed.

Hermsen & Streigel Brewing Co. Also in 1904, Hermsen and Streigel opened a little brewery at 1914 South 30th Street, but they lasted only a year.

Northwest Brewing Co. In early 1934, shortly after Repeal, the Northwest Brewery was founded at 105 East 26th Street. Northwest Brewing Co. also owned the old John Stahl brewery in Walla Walla. Two years later it was reorganized as the United Union Breweries; in 1946 it was purchased by new owners, who renamed it Pioneer Brewing–Tacoma, Inc. The plant kept that name until 1950, when it was purchased by Heidelberg Brewing Co., which then closed its Silver Springs Brewery in Port Orchard and began brewing under the Silver Springs label at the former United Union plant in Tacoma. The brewery was closed in 1967.

TEKOA

This Whitman County town near the Idaho border had a small brewery from 1908 through 1912. The Tekoa Brewing Co. was owned by partners R. Salie and F. Dirr.

TWISP

The Twisp Brewing & Malting Co. began operating in 1902, but it was out of business the next year.

UNION GAP

As most folks in Union Gap know, the town used to be called Yakima City. And Yakima City had a brewery. In fact, it had two. Pioneer Yakima Valley resident Charles Schanno established a brewery in 1878, and Abraham D. Eglin opened one in 1884. In 1879 the Schanno Brewery sold 97 barrels of beer.

In the spring of 1885, the Northern Pacific Railroad literally moved businesses and homes, including the Schanno Brewery, north from Yakima City to North Yakima, about ten miles. Later, after 1906, the "North" was dropped from the city of Yakima, and the former Yakima City became known as Union Gap. (See the Yakima listing for a continuation of the Charles Schanno Brewery.)

UNIONTOWN

There was a modest but successful brewery in this Whitman County community from 1884 to 1901. Peter Jacobs established the Union Brewery in the summer of 1884. The popular, happy German *Bräumeister* and his wife Sophie were well thought of and respected in Uniontown. One reason might have been Peter's reputation for honesty and fairness, another might have been his cheerful generosity. Take the chickens, for instance.

Herr Jacobs noticed that stray chickens showed up from time to time at the brewery, drawn by the spent malt mash grains used in brewing. The malthouse floor furnished excellent, convenient, and warm dining for the chickens and constant exercise for Peter's brewery workers in chasing them away.

After a while, however, the brewer hit upon an idea. He issued orders for chicken coops to be built adjacent to the malthouse. After that, whenever mash-hungry chickens invaded the brewery,

Peter added to his flock. He fed them all the good mash grain they could hold, and they were contented, healthy, well-fed birds.

Then came the Fourth of July, 1887, and time for the community picnic. Peter Jacobs, the friendly little brewer, was the hit of the day. He supplied not only his usual generous number of kegs filled with his best lager, but he also brought along many delicious, mash-fed roasted chickens. The tradition of Peter Jacobs' Fourth of July chickens was started on that day in 1887 and continued for some years.

Peter passed away in 1893, and his wife Sophie ran the brewery until 1897, when she took on a managing partner, Joseph Portz. In 1899 Portz bought out Sophie's interest, changed the name to Uniontown Brewery, and continued brewing for two more years. The brewery closed in 1901.

VANCOUVER

Brewing in Vancouver began in 1856 when John Muench established his brewery near Fort Vancouver in what was then Washington Territory. Muench was called "the leading brewer of the

Anton Young's Vancouver Brewery, sold by young Henry Weinhard in 1862. It became well known as the Star Brewery in 1894.

coast north of San Francisco." In the next year he hired an immigrant brewer named Henry Weinhard as an assistant. Young Henry worked for Muench only six months, then left to start his own brewery in Portland.

That same year Henry Weinhard returned to Vancouver and in 1859 bought out John Muench's interest in the Vancouver Brewery. Weinhard's beer from the small plant near the fort was sold in Portland, Astoria, The Dalles, and Walla Walla. Records show he charged 50¢ a gallon for his lager, and he sold it in kegs of five, six, eight, and ten gallons. One of the employees at the Vancouver Brewery in 1858–59 was Henry Ludwig, who by 1870 would be one of Weinhard's Portland competitors with his East Portland Brewery.

After operating the Vancouver Brewery for about three years, Weinhard sold it in 1862 to a German brewer named Anton Young and crossed back over the Columbia River to Portland, where he built a brewing empire.

When Anton Young had run the brewery at Vancouver for five years, selling his popular "Hop Gold" beer, he dismantled the plant and moved it to a better location adjacent to the public

Rear view of the Star Brewery in Vancouver at Sixth and C Streets, showing the long false-fronted cooperage. Photo circa 1895.

Some of the Star Brewery crew in 1904.

square. Here he rebuilt the structure and continued brewing under Young's Vancouver Brewery for another 27 years.

In 1894 Young sold his brewery to Louis Gerlinger, a Chicago brewer, who changed the name to Star Brewery and continued producing "Hop Gold" beer. Gerlinger greatly enlarged the plant, and he also established a sales office in Portland at 225 First Street.

Gerlinger sold the Star Brewery in 1899 to his brewmaster, Gustav Freiwald, who kept the Star name and made modern improvements to increase production of the now widely acclaimed "Hop Gold" beer.

Star Brewery was purchased in 1905 by the Northern Brewing Company, and the Sixth and Columbia plant was again enlarged and modernized with an outlay of $165,000. *Bräumeister* Adam Mueller was the manager. The capacity of the brewery in 1909 was 100,000 barrels per year, though it is doubtful that so much was actually produced in those days. The beer was shipped throughout the Northwest and south to California. Also in 1909, the Portland office of Star Brewery was moved to an ornate building at 361 East Burnside.

The Star Brewery ice plant would make thirty tons of ice daily, and the sale of ice to saloons, restaurants, hotels, and homes was a lucrative sideline for Northern Brewing.

Northern Brewing Company continued operating for eleven years, until the brewkettle was emptied by state prohibition in 1916.

Upon repeal of national Prohibition, the old Star Brewery was acquired by the Interstate Brewing Company and reopened on October 23, 1933. In 1950 the plant was purchased by George C. Norgan's Lucky Lager Brewing Co. of California, and in 1970 John Labatt, a major Canadian brewer, bought the Vancouver Lucky Lager Brewery.

The last owner of the large beer plant was General Brewing Company, which purchased Lucky Lager in October 1971. By 1978 the Vancouver brewery was the sole producer of Lucky Lager when General Brewing closed its San Francisco operation. In that same year, over 600,000 barrels of Lucky Lager beer were made at Vancouver.

In August 1985 the massive complex on the site of Anton Young's 1867 brewery was closed permanently, and the equipment was sold to a Chinese brewing firm.

Vancouver's Lucky Lager brewery, closed in recent years, occupied the site of the old Star Brewery.

Dampfhoffer Brewery. L. Dampfhoffer had a small brewery in Vancouver from 1879 to 1884. In 1879 he sold thirty barrels of beer.

Moeckel Brewery. This short-lived brewing concern ran about three years, from 1882 through 1884.

Francis & Holtmann Brewery. These partners opened a little brewery in 1884, but they were out of business by the next year.

Great Western Malting Co. Though not a brewery, Great Western Malting deserves mention because of its integral ties with the brewing industry.

In 1935, when the surviving and new breweries were going at full capacity to serve a thirsty Northwest, five men formed Great Western Malting Co. in Vancouver. Three of the five were well-known brewers: Arnold Blitz of Blitz-Weinhard; Peter Schmidt of Olympia Brewing; and Emil Sick of Sicks' Rainier Brewing Co. Bill Einzig was the manager and Morgan Kellett was the operator.

The business purpose of Great Western was to provide quality malt to breweries. As noted in Chapter Two, malt is the chief ingredient in beer. It is the primary source of beer flavor and provides the enzymes that start the brewing process.

In 1964 the management of Great Western Malting reorganized and purchased the company from the brewers.

With its long-standing policy of hiring the best maltsters and chemists, and using only first quality barley, Great Western Malting Co. has always enjoyed an excellent reputation among brewers worldwide. In addition to the main facility on West Eleventh in Vancouver, Great Western also has plants in California and Idaho. The company consistently rates among the top four malting concerns from seventeen countries.

WALLA WALLA

City Brewery. The first brewery in town was established in 1855 by pioneer brewer Emil Meyer, about whom little is recorded. It is known that he sold the brewery to John H. Stahl in 1870.

John Stahl, an experienced brewer from Germany, arrived in America in 1850, worked in breweries in California, then came north to open a brewery at Canyon City, Oregon in 1862. Eight years later he moved to Walla Walla and acquired the City Brewery.

The brewery was located at South Second and Birch Streets,

where the Eagles Club and a bowling alley are now situated. The brewery at that time consisted of a wide, rambling, one-story wooden structure. Next door to the brewery Stahl built a fine two-story brick home in 1872 for his family. The house still stands as one of the oldest brick residences in Walla Walla.

With the increasing success of his City Brewery, Stahl removed the original wood-frame building in 1880 and erected a massive brick brewery complex in its place. The new brewery included two multi-level adjoining buildings and a five-story brewhouse.

John Stahl passed away in 1884, and his wife Catherine continued the business and became very successful. From 1884 until 1912 Mrs. Stahl was sole owner of the brewery. She employed experienced brewers, many of whom had been with her husband for some time, and she personally supervised all departments of the brewery.

In an 1891 commercial guide to Walla Walla firms, Catherine Stahl was profiled thus: "Upon his decease, Mrs. Stahl, who possesses business ability much beyond the average share of women, or men either, for that matter, determined to continue the business so well established by her husband, and its proud position today among the most solid and reliable manufacturing enterprises of Walla Walla, shows her judgement to have been a wise one."

The business was reorganized as the Walla Walla Brewing Co., Inc. in 1912, and continued under that name until 1916.

Upon Repeal, the old brewery was acquired by Northwest Brewing Company, Inc., a firm that also owned a Tacoma brewery. Two years later the brewery operated under the name of United Union Breweries, Inc., and from 1945 until closing in 1952, the historic brewery started by Emil Meyer almost 100 years earlier was known as Pioneer Brewing Company of Walla Walla.

Walla Walla Brewery. The next brewing company in Walla Walla was established in 1873 by George Seisser, who sold it to Benjamin Scott four years later. Scott kept the brewery for two years. It sold 92 barrels of beer in 1876, 360 barrels in 1878, and 649 barrels in 1879.

George Gleim was the next owner of the small brick brewery on Lower Main Street, acquiring it from Scott at the end of 1879. George changed the name to Gleim's Brewery in 1881 when he hung a sign to that effect on the front of the building.

George Gleim was from Bohemia, and he decided that Walla Walla needed a polka band for the pleasure of the German residents in town. He offered six month's free beer to any civic or other group able to put together a decent polka band. Within a month Herr Gleim had his band, complete with accordion, oompah brass, and German costumes. The little group consisted of German businessmen who made their polka-playing debut right in front of the George Gleim Brewery. No doubt they enjoyed their six months' worth of unlimited free lager from George's kegs.

In 1884 Gleim sold the brewery to the Harter brothers, who used the original name, Walla Walla Brewery. The little brick brewhouse went out of business three years later.

Star Brewery. Jacob Betz was an interesting old-time brewer who made "Betz Beer" for 22 years in Walla Walla and was elected mayor five times.

Born in the Rhineland of Germany in 1843, young Jacob was apprenticed in a large brewery where he learned the brewer's and cooper's trades. Arriving in New York in 1860, the seventeen-year-old immigrant worked in breweries there and in Philadelphia and Cincinnati. Six years later he came west to San Francisco, where he worked his trade for another six years. In 1872 he and a partner owned a small brewery in San Francisco, and two years later Betz sold his interest and moved north to Walla Walla.

Arriving in the fall of 1874, the brewmaster bought the tiny, struggling Star Brewery on Main Street, between Third and Fourth Streets. Here he brewed his good lager and built up the business for seven years. In 1881 he purchased the large two-story wooden building then being used as the county courthouse. The building, on the southwest corner of Third and Alder, was remodeled and a big multilevel brick structure was joined to it in 1882.

This complex formed the nucleus of Jacob Betz's Star Brewery. On the ground floor of the brewery was a stylish saloon, and on the floor above it was a social hall for dances, meetings, and weddings.

During the next few years the Star Brewery produced about 10,000 barrels of beer annually, and shipments were made to many Northwest points. And the busy, popular brewer known as Jake Betz still had time to be elected city councilman for several terms and mayor of Walla Walla five times.

Walla Walla's Star Brewery, circa 1885.

Jake Betz moved to Tacoma in 1904, but he retained ownership of the Star Brewery, officially known as the Jacob Betz Brewing & Malting Co. In Tacoma, Jake did not engage in brewing, but became a well-known land developer and builder. He passed away in 1912, two years after finally closing his beloved Star Brewery in Walla Walla.

Kleber Brewery. F. E. Kleber operated a small brewery in Walla Walla for eight years. Born in Germany in 1830, Kleber was trained in the brewing arts there before coming to San Francisco in 1856, and then Walla Walla in 1865. In 1874 he opened his brewery, ran it until 1880, then leased it for two years to Krekel and Hinger. Kleber took over again in 1882 and brewed for two more years, finally closing in 1884.

Washington Brewery. Albert C. Ernst opened a brewery in 1882 at the east end of Main Street. His Washington Brewery ran under Ernst's control until 1885, when he sold it to H. Schwartz. The brewery was permanently closed two years later.

Hecker Brewery. Charles M. Hecker had a small brewery in Walla Walla from 1882 to 1883. Little is known about it.

Goesch & Huber Brewery. These partners owned a brewing enterprise for two years, 1891 through 1892.

WATERVILLE

The Waterville Brewery was established in 1890 by E. F. Hauch, Jr. He kept it for three years, then sold it to George L. Forschner. In 1897 Forschner sold the little brewery to its last owner, Michael Schuster, who ran it for another three years, closing in 1900.

YAKIMA

Schanno Brewery. As already mentioned in the section on Union Gap, Charles Schanno, a Yakima Valley pioneer of 1870, established the first brewery in the area four miles south of present Yakima in what was then known as Yakima City. The Northern Pacific Railroad literally moved homes and businesses, including the Schanno Brewery, north from Yakima City—some ten miles then—to a new townsite called North Yakima. Later the "North" was dropped and the city became Yakima. The old Yakima City to the south became known as Union Gap.

Five long-gone Washington labels: from left to right, "Alt Pilsener (Columbia Breweries, Tacoma); "Sicks' Select" (Seattle Brewing & Malting Co., later Rainier); "Golden Age" (Golden Age Breweries, Spokane); "Columbia Ale" (Columbia Breweries, Tacoma); "Bohemian Club" (Bohemian Breweries, Spokane).

And that's how the Schanno Brewery got from Union Gap to Yakima. Charles Schanno continued brewing beer for Yakima Valley until 1890.

Perkins & Sandmeyer Brewing Co. These partners operated a small brewery in Yakima from 1886 to 1888.

North Yakima Brewing and Malting Co. The North Yakima Brewing & Malting Co. was established in 1905 in the old Switzer's Opera House building at 25 North Front Street across from the railroad depot. The brewery was headed by J. J. Schlotfeldt, president, and the brewmaster was C. E. Wendt. The company brewed until state prohibition closed all breweries in 1916.

Upon Repeal in 1933 the brewery reopened as the Yakima Brewing and Bottling Co., and it ran until the end of 1938.

As an unusual sidelight, the old quarters of the 1905 brewery are once again host to a brewkettle and mash tun. Since 1982 the site has been occupied by Bert Grant's Yakima Brewing and Malting Co., a well-known microbrewery (see Chapter Six).

Chapter Five

Henry, Andrew, and Leopold: The Big Three

MOST OF THE BREWERIES were linked to a particular brewmaster, trained either in America or in the Old Country, in the long tradition of Pacific Northwest brewing. He was the one most closely associated with the company name, and he was the one who charted the course and kept the helm of the business, often alone.

A few breweries were controlled at the outset by corporate boards, but the lion's share of the beer produced in Oregon and Washington in the 19th century and the early years of this century was the result of the dreams and sweat of individual brewers.

Three of these historic beer plants, established long ago by their pioneer founders, are with us still, and they have grown to become the largest brewing operations in the Pacific Northwest, and among the largest in the country. We see their names daily as familiar memorials to the three old-time German brewers who created them: Henry Weinhard of Blitz-Weinhard; Andrew Hemrich of Rainier; and Leopold Schmidt of Olympia.

Henry Weinhard and the Blitz-Weinhard Story

During Henry Weinhard's early days in Portland, most streets were deep in mud or dust, and his beer wagons and horses bogged down many times. But Henry was building his reputation on good beer and dependable service, so his ads announced: "Steamboats, Steamships, Hotels, Restaurants, Saloons and Private Families furnished at their doors by leaving their orders at my office at the Brewery, or with my Driver on the Wagon."

Henry was in Portland to stay, and his brewery eventually

Henry Weinhard (1830–1904), Oregon's brew king.

grew from a dream and a ten-gallon brewkettle into a major Northwest enterprise.

Like the majority of early American brewers, Henry Weinhard learned his art in the Old Country. Born in Lindenbronn, Württemberg, Germany in 1830, young Weinhard completed his schooling and began an apprenticeship to the brewer's trade. He learned quickly, and by the time he was 22 it was recognized that Henry Weinhard was destined for a career as a master brewer.

The reports he heard about America and its opportunities led Henry to believe he might do well for himself in his chosen profession on this side of the Atlantic. In 1852 the adventurous young *Bräumeister* packed his brewing journals, notes, and recipes and emigrated to the United States.

VANCOUVER BREWERY

H. WEINHARD, Proprietor.

North First Street, Between D and E,

PORTLAND, - - - - OREGON.

The Proprietor of this well known establishment, takes pleasure in announcing to the public generally, that he is now prepared to supply their demands with the best

A No. 1 LAGER BEER,

That can be found on this Coast,

AND AT PRICES THAT DEFY COMPETITION

After many years' experience, he flatters himself that

His Beer cannot be Beat!

And that further comment is unnecessary.

Country Orders solicited and promptly filled.

CAUTION.—Customers will please notice the Brand on my Kegs, to prevent being taken in with spurious articles.

My Beer can be Shipped

To any portion of the Globe, to any Climate, and *Warranted Not to Sour*, in packages

From one Quart to One Thousand Gallons,

As desired. Also, always on hand

Good Fresh Brewers' Yeast.

H. WEINHARD.

N. B.—Steamboats, Steamships, Hotels, Restaurants, Saloons and Private Families, furnished daily at their doors, by leaving their orders at my office at the Brewery, or with my Driver on the Wagon. A liberal deduction made to the Trade—"or any other man."

H. WEINHARD.

At the time of this 1862 advertisement, Henry Weinhard was brewing beer on First Street in Portland at the brewery he purchased from Henry Saxer.

From 1852 until 1856 Weinhard was employed by a large brewery in Cincinnati, Ohio. But he was intrigued by the far West; spurred on by reports of few breweries out there, he left Cincinnati, made his way to Philadelphia, and boarded a vessel bound for the Pacific Coast by way of the Isthmus of Panama.

On a bright spring afternoon in 1856, the sailing ship brought Henry to Fort Vancouver in the Washington Territory. Franklin Pierce was president, Oregon was not yet a state, and the first rumblings of the Civil War were yet to be heard.

Outside the fort was a small brewery recently established by John Muench. Henry worked for Muench's Vancouver Brewery for about six months while he adjusted to the new country. Then he left Vancouver and moved south to the new, growing settlement on the Willamette River, near the junction of the Columbia. At that time (1856), Portland had a population of about 1,200. Just the year before it had been made the county seat for Multnomah County, and because of its advantageous position geographically it was predicted that Portland would soon usurp Oregon City as the area's commercial center.

In the late fall, Henry went into partnership with George Bottler in a small brewery at present Couch and Front Streets, near the river. But as the weeks passed, the expected profit and growth of the business did not develop as rapidly as Henry had hoped, so he returned to Vancouver in early 1857. Two years later Weinhard bought John Muench's interest in the Vancouver Brewery and was content to brew beer there for a while, keeping an eye on burgeoning Portland.

After a little over three years of running the brewery near Fort Vancouver, Henry sold the company in 1862 to a German brewer named Anton Young and moved back across the Columbia

In 1863 Henry Weinhard purchased land at the present 12th and Burnside site and built his City Brewery, pictured here. Photo from an 1864 business directory.

Advertisement for City Brewery, circa 1882.

to Portland. He purchased Henry Saxer's brewery, at present First and Davis Streets, and still maintained a connection with George Bottler.

In 1863 Henry Weinhard bought property away from the center of town, with only a single road into the place, and here he built his new brewery. It was on the same site where Blitz-Weinhard stands today. He called his new enterprise the City Brewery, and housed it in a neat wood-frame building. This time his business was successful, and in time he had to expand his facilities. More wooden structures went up, including a large home adjacent to the brewery, where Henry lived with his wife Louise and their children.

By 1870 Henry Weinhard's City Brewery was a well established, profitable Portland business, about whose product the

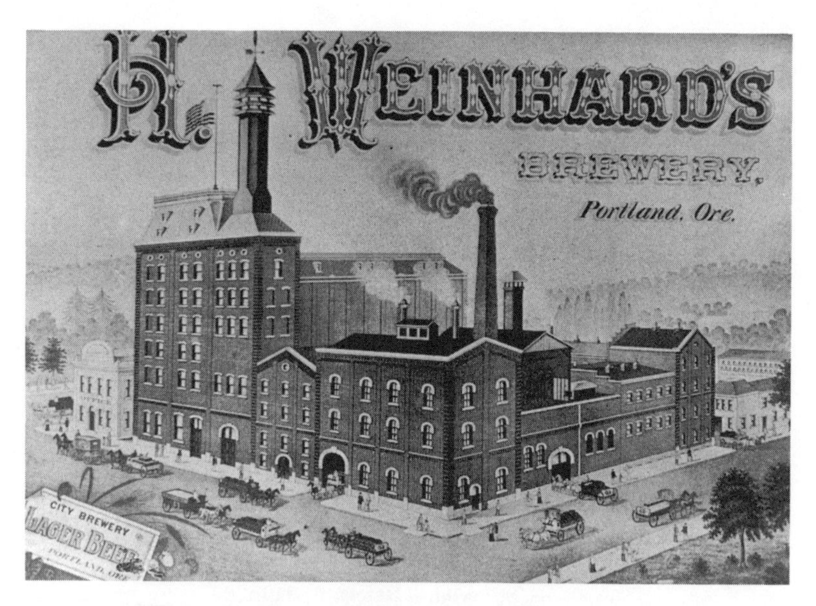

Some early Pacific Northwest breweries, such as Henry Weinhard's City Brewery, were showplaces of industrial architecture. The massive structure, castle-like turrets, and lofty brewhouse towers gave them a stately appearance.

proprietor could boast in ads: "My beer can be shipped to any portion of the globe, to any climate, and warranted not to sour." At that time the brewery was producing over 2,000 barrels of beer annually.

The brewery in 1882 was the largest in the Pacific Northwest, but its pioneer founder wanted a "monument to brewing." In that year the frame building came down and in its place rose what Oregon historian H. K. Hines called "an immense pile of brick, which covers the entire block," at what is now 12th and West Burnside. The massive brick brewhouse was the nucleus of a complex of brewery structures that extended from 11th to 13th Streets. The bottling department was located across Couch Street, by federal law, on the west side of the brewery. The stables for the teams of beer-wagon horses were on 13th Street, and a large warehouse was maintained at the steamboat dock.

Henry Weinhard, the wealthy brewer, was also Weinhard the philanthropist. His personal friendliness and generosity won acclaim among charitable organizations, and he was a sure touch for any civic program needing funding. As an example of the Henry Weinhard that Portland came to love, there is the Skidmore Fountain story. In 1887 druggist Steven Skidmore passed away. In his will was a bequest of $5,000 for the construction of a large ornate drinking fountain to be placed in the business part of the city, "that dogs and work horses and thirsty laboring men might have drink."

Charles E. S. Wood, Oregon writer, painter, and attorney, took on the project of overseeing the building of the beautiful Skidmore Fountain at present Southwest First and Ankeny. The fountain was completed in September 1888, and Wood was planning the unveiling ceremony. He also happened to be Henry Weinhard's attorney. One day Henry came to see him on what Wood supposed was legal business. "But when we were alone," wrote Wood in a 1904 *Oregonian* item, "Henry unbosomed himself of the proposition that he himself would bear the expense of whatever hose was necessary, in addition to the fire hose of the city, to connect his largest lager tank with the fountain and have the fountain spout free beer."

Free beer at the unveiling ceremony of the Skidmore Fountain!

Henry Weinhard offered to run beer through Skidmore Fountain at its dedication in 1888.

What an idea! Wood thanked Henry and conveyed the proposition to the city fathers. Alas, it was not to be. It was almost one mile on busy city streets from the brewery to the fountain, and they were afraid there would be so many hose punctures along the way made by beer-loving pranksters that little of the foamy brew would reach the fountain ceremonies. So attorney Wood thanked Henry Weinhard sincerely for his offer and told him the city was obliged to decline.

The Weinhard beer output in 1890 had increased to 40,000 barrels a year. The company had many commercial customers all along the Pacific Coast and in other Western states and territories, and a lot of City Brewery beer was also exported overseas to China, Japan, the Philippines, and Siberia. Henry also kept the major share of the Portland beer market, supplying his product by wagon delivery and through Weinhard-owned saloons, such as the Hof Bräu, the Oregon Grille, the Quelle Bar, the Headquarters Saloon on Alder Street, and the Germania Saloon on the west side of First, between Oak and Pine. The Germania even had one of the first telephones in town for direct placement of large beer orders to the brewery.

Life in Weinhard's City Brewery during the 1890s was good.

One of Henry Weinhard's beer delivery wagons, about 1900.

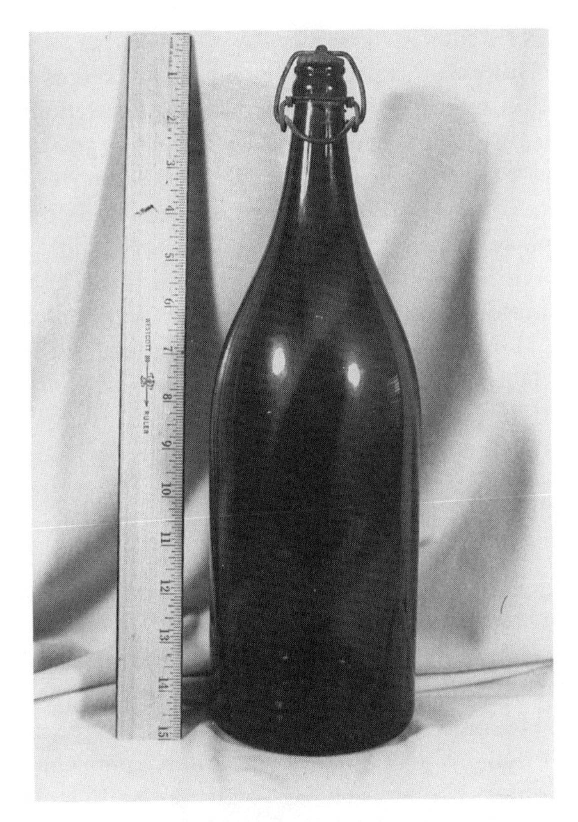

This early 1900s Henry Weinhard beer bottle, called a "picnic," stood nearly 15″ high and held two quarts of Henry's finest. Notice the old-style stopper.

Henry offered excellent job security and a generous wage of $15 to $18 a week, with overtime paid at 50¢ an hour. A clause in the 1891 United Brewery Workmen contract stated: "In case dullness of the trade necessitates a reduction of the working force, the men shall be laid off in an impartial way in rotation. No man shall be laid off longer or less than one week at a time."

The brewery workday was nine hours, starting at 6 a.m., except for the brewkettle men who were needed earlier, and all the workers were at the job six days a week. One unusual fringe benefit was that beer was given free of charge to employees during working hours.

At the turn of the century Henry Weinhard was truly Oregon's brew king. His massive brewery, by then known as the Henry Weinhard Brewery, was producing 100,000 barrels of beer annually, and "Columbia" beer was well-known throughout the West and in worldwide markets. He constructed large ice plants in Eugene and Roseburg in place of the local breweries he bought out, and there were Weinhard beer storage buildings in those towns as well as in Oregon City, Baker, Medford, and Aberdeen.

Henry Weinhard died on September 20, 1904. The brewery remained under family control as brewery superintendent Paul Wessinger, Henry's son-in-law, took over as head of the business. The name Henry Weinhard Brewery was retained, and "Columbia" was still the chief brand.

When the lights of most breweries went dark in 1916, the Weinhard Brewery stayed afloat through the efforts of Paul Wessinger and, later, his son Henry. They allowed the historic plant to survive Prohibition by making soft drinks, such as sarsaparilla, ginger and birch beers, and fruit drinks, syrups, flavorings, and toppings. They also made a malt extract for cooking. It was a far cry from the days of brewing thousands of barrels of "Columbia" beer, but at least the doors of the big brick building at 12th and Burnside were never closed.

The Prohibition years brought another major change to the Henry Weinhard Brewery. Henry Wessinger could feel the end to the dry years approaching in 1927. With the hope of a bright brewing future just over the horizon, Wessinger entered into a deal designed for profitability and a reduction of competition.

The two largest brewing concerns in Portland at the time were the Weinhard plant and the Portland Brewing Company, run by Arnold I. Blitz. The two giants decided on a merger, the new company to be called the Blitz-Weinhard Brewing Company. Arnold Blitz was made president and Henry Wessinger was vice president. Fred H. Rothchild, Blitz's partner at Portland Brewing, was a director, as was John A. Laring.

The *Oregonian* announced the news on the morning of January 13, 1928:

BREWERIES TO COMBINE

Consolidation of the brewing activities of Portland's two largest breweries, the Henry Weinhard plant and the Portland Brewing Company, and the organization of the Blitz-Weinhard Company to control more than half a million dollars' worth of properties, has been completed, according to an announcement made last night by John A. Laring, attorney for the Henry Weinhard estate.

A. I. Blitz, ex-president of the Portland Brewing Company, will act as president and manager; Henry Wessinger as vice-president, and the directors will include John A. Laring and F. H. Rothchild.

Negotiations looking toward the consolidation have been under way for several months. Its completion presages the extension of the markets of the two concerns into all parts of the Pacific Northwest and into new territory in the intermountain regions.

The Weinhard plant has operated as a separate unit for more than half a century, and the Portland Brewing Company for approximately half that length of time.

Under the new arrangement all the Columbia and Blitz brews and other draught beverages will be produced at the Blitz-Weinhard plant at Twentieth and Upshur streets. All bottled products heretofore produced by the consolidated concerns including Blitz and Columbia brews, will be bottled at the Weinhard plant. The Henry Weinhard Company will continue to manufacture and distribute other lines as in the past. These will include fruit syrups and soda fountain supplies.

The Weinhard plant occupies several blocks of ground between Tenth and Fourteenth streets, and Couch and Burnside. A portion of the property fronting on Burnside, it is said, will be converted into commercial uses.

Construction of additional buildings and the installation of new equipment have already been started by the Blitz-Weinhard Company at Twentieth and Upshur streets.

Pending completion of the additions, both companies will continue to manufacture independently, but this, it is expected, will be for less than six weeks.

When the repeal of Prohibition put life in America's brewkettles again, Blitz-Weinhard was ready. With the addition of Arnold Blitz's former Portland Brewing plant at 20th and Upshur, the merged operation set new sales records in the late 1930s. The chief advertising campaign was built around a slogan reminding everyone who the founder was: "Guaranteed satisfying—from the private recipe of Henry Weinhard."

During World War II, beer available to civilians was limited and there was an acute beer shortage in some sections of the country. Breweries, including Blitz-Weinhard, agreed to hold back at least fifteen percent of their output to supply the armed services first.

In the mid-1930s, Blitz-Weinhard beer was available in clear or brown 11-ounce bottles.

It was not uncommon for crowds to be lined up at Oregon and Washington taverns waiting for the first delivery of the day—and a few rationed glasses of cold, refreshing beer.

After 1953, when Sicks' Brewing Co. closed its Salem plant, Blitz-Weinhard was the only brewery in Oregon. The company was still controlled by Weinhard and Blitz family members: Henry Wessinger, a Weinhard grandson, was chairman of the board, and two of the founder's great-grandsons, Fred and William Wessinger, were vice presidents. William F. Blitz, son of Arnold, was also a vice president.

By the 1960s Fred and William Wessinger had assumed the helm as president and chairman of the board. They brought the company to its apex by selling one-third of all beer bought in

Oregon. One of the Wessinger's proud successes during that time was "Olde English Malt Liquor." Californians were quaffing Blitz brew in the 1960s, and it was offered to the East Coast in the early 1970s. And the brothers' introduction of "Henry Weinhard's Private Reserve" in 1974 proved to be one of the all-time success stories of America's latter-day brewing industry.

Other Blitz-Weinhard brands, in addition to their main-label brews, were "Alta," "Cascade," and "Buffalo." They also produced "Aspen Gold" and "Golden Velvet" under contract to the Trivoli Brewing Co. of Denver.

In 1977 Blitz-Weinhard was America's fifteenth-oldest brewery. But the year 1979 marked an end to one of the last independent breweries. On January 31 of that year the *Oregonian* announced the sale of Blitz-Weinhard to Milwaukee's oldest brewery, the Pabst Brewing Company, founded in 1844. The changeover was effective on April 1, 1979, and for the first time Henry Weinhard's old beer plant was out of family control, although the Wessingers continued to manage it.

The new change in ownership brought a multi-million-dollar expansion to the Burnside brewery, with separate facilities at the plant for brewing Blitz-Weinhard and Pabst beers.

Four years later, in 1983, another change of ownership took place with the acquisition of Pabst by the G. Heileman Brewing Co. of La Crosse, Wisconsin. And in 1988 G. Heileman was bought by an Australian company, Bond Corp. Holdings, Ltd., for $1.27 billion.

Blitz-Weinhard now employs about 350 people and is managed by Bruce Vaughan. Robert Weisskirchen is the brewmaster. The plant brews 1.2 million barrels of beer and ale annually. Tours of the brewery are conducted Monday through Friday at 1:00 p.m., 2:30 p.m., and 4:00 p.m.

The brewery at 12th and Burnside has come a long way from the days when Henry Weinhard brewed in a ten-gallon copper kettle. And it might just be that the old master would not have minded all the growth and changes. After all, it's been good for business.

Andrew Hemrich and His "Rainier Beer"

When young Andrew Hemrich was working long days learning the brewer's trade in his father's Alma, Wisconsin brewery, he could not have known that one day he would command a colossal conglomerate of breweries far away in the Pacific Northwest.

Andrew was a first-generation American, born to a German immigrant brewer named John Hemrich in 1856. Growing up at his father's brewery, Andrew and his younger brothers, Alvin and Louis, gained an intimate knowledge of brewing methods before they were in their mid-teens. At the age of fourteen Andrew left home and went to the wild mining regions of the West, spending twelve years in Colorado, Nevada, Idaho, and Montana. Wherever he roamed, when the opportunity came up, he worked in a brewery.

After arriving in Montana when he was twenty years old, Andrew established his own small brewery at Glendale, which he operated successfully for several years. He then sold his plant and took a position as superintendent of the Bozeman Brewing Company. At the end of two years in Bozeman, Hemrich made a decision that would set him on the path to his destiny. Formulating plans with a brewer friend named John Kopp, a young German immigrant, Andrew counted his stake of $1,500, resigned his position, and left for the boisterous frontier lumber town of Seattle, Washington Territory, to open a brewery.

When Andrew Hemrich arrived in Seattle on February 18, 1883, the booming town was wide open and had a population of about 7,000. With John Kopp, Andrew selected and purchased a piece of property south of town at what would later be Ninth Avenue South (now Airport Way South) and Hanford. The site was situated snug against a hill with a view of mighty Mount Rainier in the background.

Here the two young brewers constructed several wood-frame buildings and opened their Bay View Brewery under the firm name of Kopp & Hemrich. Andrew chose to name their first batch of beer after the huge mountain that dominated the view to the southeast. They began brewing half a barrel of "Rainier" beer each day. The recipe used at Bay View produced a popular brew, and by the end of the first year the newcomers had sold 200 barrels of beer.

Andrew Hemrich's early Bay View Brewery, shown here in 1886, grew into a large consolidation of breweries and finally became Rainier Brewing Company.

The Kopp-Hemrich partnership lasted only two years. At the end of 1884 Andrew bought out John Kopp's interest and, joined in business by his father, John Hemrich, reorganized the brewery and incorporated it as the Bay View Brewing Company, Inc.

In June 1889 the devastating Great Seattle Fire swept through the downtown district of the city, wiping out virtually the entire core area. By the time the fire was out, 58 blocks—116 acres—were destroyed. The Bay View Brewery was spared because of its location well south of the fire area.

Andrew and his father quickly offered their services to the community in whatever ways were necessary. They sent men from the brewhouse to help fight the fire and assist in clearing rubble, and they brought barrels of their finest lager to the fatigued firefighters. They also set up free beer stands at the emergency tent shelters where dispossessed men and women congregated to sleep and get a meal.

John Hemrich retired in 1890, and two years later a major reorganization took place at the Hemrich plant. Andrew and his brother-in-law, Frederick Kirschner, arranged a complicated merger agreement between the Hemrich family and a number of other brewery owners, and a new, gigantic entity came into being, the Seattle Brewing & Malting Company. The new beer giant absorbed three major breweries: the Albert Braun Brewing Association; the Claussen-Sweeney Brewing Co.; and Hemrich's Bay View Brewing Company. All three breweries continued to operate, only now they were under the Seattle Brewing & Malting banner. The Claussen-Sweeney branch brewery was located in a large brick building in the Georgetown district, two miles south of the Bay View Brewery. The Braun Brewery was in another part of town.

Andrew Hemrich was joined by his brothers Alvin, Louis, and John Jr. in managing all Seattle Brewing & Malting holdings. Andrew was elected president of the corporation and remained in that office until he died.

By this time, all of Andrew's younger brothers were experienced brewers. Like Andrew, Alvin and Louis had been raised at their father's brewery in Alma, Wisconsin. Alvin later opened his own brewery in Durand, Wisconsin, and still later was manager of

An 1898 view of Andrew Hemrich's headquarters brewery, the Seattle Brewing & Malting Co. The site at 3100 Airport Way South is now the home of the modern Rainier Brewing Company.

A few of the Seattle Brewing & Malting Co. crew pose to advertise their "Rainier Beer."

the Victoria Brewing Co. in British Columbia. Louis had worked for Andrew at the Bay View Brewery for four years, as had John Junior.

Seattle Brewing & Malting acquisitions continued through the 1890s to the turn of the century. In 1897 the historic North Pacific Brewery came into the "House of Hemrich," and in 1901 the conglomerate picked up the Standard Brewing Company.

Through the years of growth and change, the Bay View Brewery was the headquarters plant of Seattle Brewing & Malting, and that's where Andrew Hemrich maintained his offices and home. Rainier Beer, produced at Bay View, was still the principal label of the company. The Rainier slogan was: "There's new vigor and strength in every drop."

The next big change in the Hemrichs' brewing life came in 1904 when a colossal new brick structure was built at 6004 Duwamish Avenue, an extension of Ninth Avenue South, in Georgetown. The nucleus of the new main plant was the former Claussen-Sweeney brewery at that site. The brewing facility was two miles south of the Bay View, on the same street (now Airport Way South). The building, three blocks long with a number of adjoining structures, took nearly three years to construct. When it was finished in late 1904 Seattle Brewing & Malting Co. had a new home, complete with an adjacent, ornate corporate office building.

The new brewery had an annual output of 300,000 barrels of beer, an amount that would double within six years. Rainier Beer was as famous in the West as Pabst and Schlitz were in the Midwest and East. The Hemrichs sent their beer to thousands of domestic commercial customers and to outlets worldwide.

Andrew Hemrich, the founder and guiding innovator of the Seattle Brewing & Malting Co. empire, died at his home on May 2, 1910 at the young age of 54.

By 1914 Seattle Brewing & Malting, still headed by the Hemrich brothers, was the largest industrial enterprise in the state of Washington and the sixth largest brewery in the United States. But two years later the lights were turned off at all the company facilities with the advent of state prohibition in 1916. The plants were closed and the Georgetown brewery was turned into a feedlot. Rights to use the coveted Rainier brand name were sold to a brewery in California, and the Hemrich brothers went into other businesses. Alvin operated the Supply Laundry Company and an

The 1904 Seattle Brewing & Malting Co. brewery in Georgetown, looking north.

This is the way Rainier Beer was bottled by the
Seattle Brewing & Malting Co. in 1914.

ice house, among other enterprises. Louis had accumulated a number of business properties, including a profitable business block in the Ballard district of Seattle, and he owned a vast acreage of valuable timber lands, all of which provided an excellent income.

With Repeal in 1933 came a tide of optimism for the rejuvenated brewing industry. The Pacific Northwest was thirsty for real, legal beer and the Hemrichs were ready to supply it. They could no longer brew and sell Rainier Beer because their original brand name was now owned by a San Francisco brewery 800 miles away.

But with the spirit that personified the Hemrich tradition, they started anew. The former Bay View Brewery was reopened as the Apex Brewing Company, producing "Apex" beer. They also established the Western Brewing Co., under the corporate umbrella of the Hemrich Investment Corp., at 5225 East Marginal Way.

Though Western Brewing lasted until 1940, the Hemrichs sold the old Seattle Brewing & Malting plant in Georgetown in 1933, and in 1935 they sold the Apex Brewery.

The purchasers of both the Seattle Brewing & Malting plant in Georgetown, and the Apex Brewery at Ninth Avenue South and Hanford, were a father-and-son brewing team, Fritz and Emil Sick. The Sick name was to become well known in the Pacific Northwest for over thirty years.

Fritz Sick was a brewer from the Old Country who immigrated to Canada by way of the Pacific Coast of the United States. His son, Emil George, was born in Tacoma in 1894. By 1902 the first Sick family brewery on this side of the Atlantic, Lethbridge Breweries, Ltd., was in operation in southwest Alberta.

As a young boy, Emil Sick learned the brewer's art at his father's side, and as he gained experience he began to take on responsible brewing positions. In 1919 he became secretary of the firm and two years later was named assistant manager. By 1928 he was managing director of the consolidation of breweries known as Associated Breweries of Canada.

In 1933 Emil moved to Seattle, where he purchased, with his father, the Hemrichs' Georgetown plant. Now owners of Seattle Brewing & Malting Co., the Sicks set about the task of returning Rainier Beer to its original home. They began what was to be a several-year-long series of financial negotiations with the California brewery that held the name.

Meanwhile, the Sicks acquired the Hemrich brothers' old Bay View Brewery, now brewing Apex Beer. The structures were torn down, and in their place rose one of the most modern post-Prohibition breweries in the country. It became the new headquarters for the Sicks' Seattle Brewing & Malt Company. The plant stands today at 3100 Airport Way South as the Rainier Brewing Company.

While waiting for the acquisition of the Rainier label, Emil Sick, president of Seattle Brewing & Malting, began brewing and bottling "Rheinlander" and "Highlander" beers.

In 1938 Emil also bought the George Horluck Brewing Company at 606 Westlake Avenue in Seattle. Operation of this

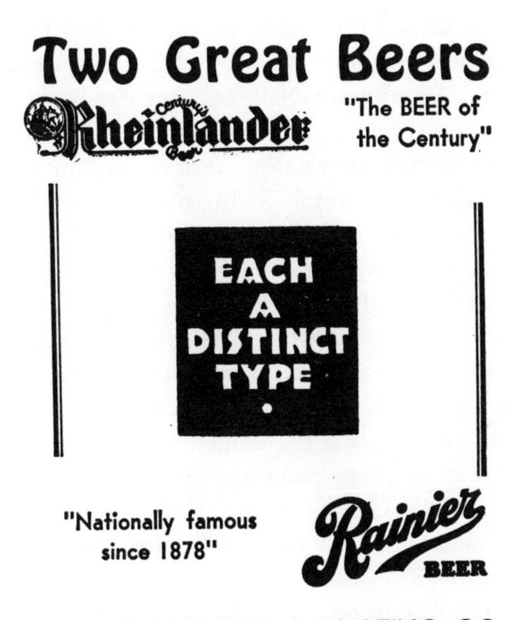

A 1936 ad proclaiming two of many brands produced by the Seattle Brewing & Malting Co.

plant continued until 1957 under the name of Sicks' Century Brewery.

Though Emil Sick had called Seattle home since 1933, he kept active in Canadian brewing and acquired other American breweries as well. By 1937 Sick was not only the president of his Seattle plants, but he held that same position with Lethbridge Breweries; Edmonton Breweries, Ltd., Edmonton, Alberta; the Regina Brewing Co. in Saskatchewan; and the Prince Albert Breweries, Ltd. of Prince Albert, Saskatchewan. He also headed the Great Falls Breweries, Inc. and the Missoula Brewing Co. in Montana.

By 1938 Sicks' Seattle Brewing & Malting Co. had repurchased the Rainier brand name, and "Rainier Beer" once again became the company's premier product.

Emil Sick celebrated the return of Rainier Beer by buying the Seattle Indians baseball team and renaming them the Rainiers. He built them a new home, Sicks' Seattle Stadium, in Rainier Valley east of the brewery. The Rainiers had been a floundering team, but with the new spark they were an instant success, winning Pacific Coast league pennants in 1939, '40, '41, '51, and '55. The team was sold to the Boston Red Sox in 1961.

With the desire to expand the range of his Pacific Northwest brewery, Emil bought the Salem Brewery Association plant in 1943 and the Spokane Breweries facilities the next year. His "Sicks' Select Beer," brewed in Salem and Spokane as well as in Seattle, became extremely popular and for some years was rated second only to Rainier Beer among the Sicks' products. The Salem brewery ran until 1953, and the Spokane branch was closed in 1962.

In 1957 Emil changed the name of Seattle Brewing & Malting Co. to Sicks' Rainier Brewing Company.

Emil Sick died in 1964, and the administration of Rainier Brewing went to his adopted son, Alan B. Ferguson. During this time the firm was undergoing other changes too. The majority stockholder in Rainier since the mid-1950s was Molson Breweries, Ltd. of Canada, the oldest brewing company in North America.

The Rainier Brewing Co. was sold by Molson in 1977 to the G. Heileman Brewing Co. of La Crosse, Wisconsin for $8 million. Heileman's reputation for fostering the development of regional beers helped Rainier attain new production and sales peaks. In 1978 Rainier's production reached one million barrels for the first time, and in 1984 more than two million barrels of beer were brewed on Airport Way under the big red *R*.

Then, in September 1987, G. Heileman announced a buyout of the company, including the Rainier plant, for $1.25 billion by the Bond Corp. Holdings, Ltd. of Australia.

Rainier Brewing Co. employs about 550 people, with John H. Lindsay as manager and Robert Magruder as brewmaster. In addition to "Rainier Beer" and "Rainier Ale," the brewery also makes "Rainier Light Beer," "Rainier Special Dry," "Colt .45," "Mickey's Ale," "Rheinlander Beer," "Schmidt Beer," "Heileman's Special Export Beer," "Bohemian Club," and "Carling Black Label." Free tours of the plant are offered from 1 p.m. to 6 p.m., Monday through Friday, excluding holidays.

The former pre-Prohibition Seattle Brewing & Malting Co. buildings in Georgetown at 6004 Airport Way South are worth a look too. With the exception of some warehouse space and a cold storage and ice company, the massive brick buildings with signs proclaiming "Brew House," "Malt House," "Stock House," and "General Offices," are mostly empty and quiet now. The hustle and noise and life of the great Seattle Brewing & Malting Co. have long faded, and the cobblestone loading area, smooth-worn from countless hooves and beer-wagon wheels, is today untrod. The imposing curbside structures that shade the narrow street fronting them patiently await their destiny, inhabited only by ghosts of a former time.

And back up the street about two miles is the giant complex where once stood the little Bay View Brewery. Andrew Hemrich would not recognize the place now, though he would no doubt approve. For when he brewed his first one-half barrel of "Rainier Beer," he started the whole thing.

Leopold Schmidt of Olympia — "It's the Water"

While on a business trip to Olympia, Washington in the fall of 1895, a friendly 49-year-old man with a slight German accent happened into a barbershop. He told the barber he was a brewer from Butte, Montana and was visiting Washington as a member of the Montana State Capital Commission.

As he sat in the chair, the man from Montana listened with great interest as the barber told him about the water from locally popular artesian wells. Soon after his haircut the visitor refreshed himself from an artesian well recently drilled by the Talcott brothers. Impressed by the crystal purity of the water, he wandered about the area and located springs of similarly potable water at nearby Tumwater.

There was property available for purchase at the springs, and after having the water tested by a laboratory the man decided to build a modest brewery on the site. His name was Leopold F. Schmidt, and his modest little beer plant would become the great Olympia Brewing Company.

Leopold Schmidt had been a brewer for twenty years before coming to Washington. He was born January 23, 1846 in Dornassenheim, Oberhessen, Germany on the Rhine River. His early education was in the schools of his native land, and when he was fourteen he went to sea, sailing the coffee route between North and South America. In the spring of 1866 he landed in New York and decided to stay in the United States. He worked on Great Lakes grain ships between Chicago and Buffalo, and on those voyages he learned the English language.

In 1868 Leopold went to the gold country of Montana and worked as a carpenter and sluice-box builder. Three years later, in Butte, he became a naturalized citizen of the United States.

It was not until 1875, at the age of 29, that Leopold became a brewer. In that year he was asked to manage the Valiton Brewery in nearby Deer Lodge, and he ran the plant successfully for a year until it was sold. But that short introduction to the brewer's life led to a new career for the popular carpenter.

Leopold joined the former Valiton brewmaster, Mr. Sallie, in a partnership, and together they opened the Centennial Brewery & Pioneer Malt House in Butte.

Finding himself even more intrigued with the business, Leopold returned to Germany in 1878 to attend the world-famous brewing academy at Worms. There he met and married Johanna Steiner, returning with her to Butte in 1879. Their son Peter, who would have much to do with his father's future Washington brewing enterprise, was born in a Butte log cabin in 1880.

Using his new scientific training in the brewing arts, Leopold introduced the first two varieties of brewing barley ever grown in Montana—grain that is still popular there. Mr. Sallie retired, selling his partnership interest to Daniel Gamer, a friend of Leopold. Mr. Schmidt was now president of Centennial Brewing Company, and it became one of Montana's most successful firms. Leopold was Butte's pioneer brewer, and he continued making good lager beer in that city until 1895. It was in the fall of that year that he visited Olympia.

After being impressed by the water and buying property at the Tumwater springs, Leopold sold his Montana brewery and moved his family to Washington.

It was now winter, hardly the best season for construction in western Washington. But slowly the small brewery took shape on a narrow bench of land below a hill, at the water's edge on placid Deschutes Inlet. Near the brewery site, the little Deschutes River flowed into the inlet; a short distance upstream, Tumwater Falls tumbled and danced on the rocks.

Leopold bought the first copper brewkettle and refrigeration equipment in Chicago, where they had been displayed at the 1893 World's Fair. Hand-formed sixteen-foot staves were made into tight, well-constructed beer tanks. Leopold chose the brewery employees, equipment, and ingredients with great care, because he was determined to brew a beer worthy of his excellent artesian water.

Finally the little brewery was ready, and Leopold Schmidt dubbed it the Capital Brewing Company. The first brewing began in July 1896. After the beer was finished aging in storage (lagering), it was siphoned by hand from wooden barrels, bottled, and put on the market by the first of October. The Capital Brewing Company's first brand was "Olympia Pale Export," and when it went to market a Pacific Northwest brewing tradition was born.

The usual price at that time for a 31-gallon barrel of beer was $3.25. The breweries had little operating margin, since that price included one dollar for federal tax. Leopold balked, insisting that

Leopold Schmidt's original Capital Brewing Company, circa 1898, on Deschutes Inlet at Lower Tumwater Falls.

his premium beer, made with precise attention and care and brewed with his superb artesian water, should command a higher price. His competitors in Seattle, Tacoma, and Portland were stunned when he asked $8.00 a barrel for his beer. He not only got his price, but the popularity of Olympia Pale Export was instantaneous, and within three months 3,500 barrels of the good brew were sold.

An early distinction of Leopold Schmidt's Capital Brewery was the type of bottle closure used. Within a few months of operation, the brewer knew that for his beer to be shipped any great distance he would have to find a better method of pasteurization to halt the continuing yeast action. So that the beer would not sour on long ocean voyages to foreign markets, it had to be subjected to heat of 142–146° F. for thirty minutes. The usual cork stoppers would not allow for this process, so Schmidt became the first Northwest brewer to use the newly invented metal crown cap for sealing the bottles.

By 1898 the products of the Capital Brewing Co. were well known and popular in the Pacific Northwest and along the West Coast. Far-ranging markets, including points overseas, were accumulating on Leopold's growing list of customers, and the Tumwater brewer was ever mindful of imaginative advertising opportunities.

When Admiral Dewey, commanding his flagship *Olympia,* defeated the Spanish fleet, bringing an end to the Spanish-American War of 1898, the citizens of Washington chipped in for a gift of a magnificent silver service to be used in the officers' wardroom aboard the *Olympia.* The lower-ranking sailors were not allowed to use the silver service, however, and when Leopold Schmidt found out he immediately sent six barrels packed with bottles of Olympia Pale Export to the crew. He also sent cases of beer, with his compliments, to many gatherings and public celebrations.

And the list of happy customers continued to grow.

John Miller Murphy, editor of the Olympia *Standard,* wrote this about Leopold and his beer: "One of the most helpful enterprises for our community, one that brings the most money from abroad, to place it in circulation in our midst, is the Capital Brewery. Its trade is extended wherever the merits of its products become known. It is unqualifiedly the best beer made on the

Olympia Beer was popular in the Klondike at an inflated 25¢ a glass.

Pacific Coast and that is saying much. In the estimation of many it fairly rivals the famous Milwaukee product."

Leopold Schmidt, with his good sense of public relations, then chose as a name for one of his beers, "Olympian Standard Beer." Not only was it a fine name for a fine beer, it also happened to be a combination of the names of the capital city's two newspapers, the *Olympian* and Murphy's *Standard.* Murphy liked to say thereafter that the name of his paper appeared on every bottle of Leopold's beer.

During this time a number of changes and expansions were going on at the brewery. The increasing popularity of Olympia Beer brought necessary enlargements of the fermenting and lagering vats, and new refrigeration equipment was added.

A pre-1902 advertising placard showing the name Capital Brewing Co.

Another factor that led to the growth of Capital Brewing at this time was the rush for gold in the Yukon. Thousands of gold-seekers flocked to the Klondike River starting in the late summer of 1897, when the outside world received news of fabulous strikes. And Olympia Beer went with them. As the Far North boomtowns of Skagway, Dyea, Dawson, and Grand Forks swelled with miners, Olympia Beer was one of the most advertised, and it was available at Far North prices: 25¢ a glass (the usual price of a 16-ounce glass of beer in the States was 5¢).

Soon there was additional expansion at the brewery as men and equipment operated at full capacity to fill big shipments of beer to the North, as well as to new markets in Hawaii and Japan.

A wharf was built at the brewery so that cases of beer could be barged to waiting ocean-going vessels at the Olympia docks and to rail cars at the freight yards. Also, electric trolleys and flatcars were used to pull loads of beer from Tumwater to Olympia on streetcar tracks.

In 1900 Leopold's oldest son, Peter, was appointed brewmaster and plant superintendent following his graduation from brewer's school in Milwaukee.

Two years later, the brewery advertising manager, Frank Kenney, proposed a slogan designed to tell people why Olympia Beer was distinctive. After much discussion and consideration, Leopold and Peter concurred with Kenney, and "It's the Water" became the official company slogan. It remains so today.

Several months after the adoption of the famous slogan, the brewery's name was changed legally from Capital Brewing Co. to Olympia Brewing Co. That same year, 1902, a further expansion increased the plant's capacity for making Olympia beer.

In 1903 Leopold Schmidt built a brewery at Bellingham and that same year purchased the Salem Brewery in Oregon. Six years later he bought the small Port Townsend Brewery. During this time he also established the Acme Brewery in San Francisco. At all of these branch breweries, the same barley, hops, yeast, and cereal adjuncts of corn and rice were used. But the Olympia brewmasters, who traveled among the scattered plants, could not produce beer comparable to that brewed in the home brewery at Tumwater. The only difference, they felt, was the water used for brewing. The water available at the other four plants, though good, was not of the same excellence as the artesian well water at Tumwater. This is why none of the beer made at the other locations ever carried the Olympia beer label.

By 1905 the need for a massive restructuring of the Olympia Brewing Co. buildings was recognized. In that year Leopold contracted with a noted brewery equipment and design firm, the Vilter Mfg. Co. of Milwaukee, Wisconsin, to design and build a large brewing plant on the site of the original wooden brewery at Tumwater. The new roomy structures were completed in 1906. The tall, stately brick brewhouse and some of the buildings still stand today, about a hundred yards north of the present plant.

At this time, six years into the 20th century, Leopold Schmidt was a well-known brewer in the Pacific Northwest. He was producing 45,000 barrels of beer a year, and his brewery was one of the largest employers in the Olympia area.

Another placard, this one from after the 1902
name change to Olympia Brewing Co.

Leopold, always the progressive businessman, traveled widely throughout the United States seeking new marketing opportunities and taking the pulse of the industry. The brewer from Tumwater was a devout family man who enjoyed offering brewery jobs to his own sons, as well as the sons of other Olympia families. He felt the brewer's art was an honorable trade to be pursued with pride and respect, and to that end he paid the highest wages in the area. Brewery employees received $4.00 per day, while good rates in town ranged from $1.35 to $2.50 a day.

Brewer Schmidt also kept a watchful eye on his brewery. He was in the habit of taking walks through the plant, chatting with employees, and assuring himself that the operation was clean, smooth and in keeping with his sense of things done right. And he detested waste.

His son Frank often told a story concerning some rusty nails. At the time, Frank Schmidt was the company purchasing agent, and one day, while he was in a discussion with one of the brewmasters, Henry Henius, in the cooperage shop, Leopold strolled through. He came across a scattering of rusty nails at the back of the cooperage and paused to pick them up. Then *Bräumeister* Schmidt approached Frank and Henius and asked them why they hadn't picked up the nails. The men replied that they felt they had more important things to do. To that Frank's father said sternly, "Well, you know, it was by picking up rusty nails like these that I built this brewery. Think that over."

By 1908 the bottle shop at Olympia Brewing was producing anywhere from 40,000 to 80,000 bottles of Olympia Beer each day.

Two tragedies struck the Olympia Brewing Co. in 1914. The year had been going well for the company, with annual production topping 100,000 barrels, but Leopold, devastated by the loss

Schmidt's brewery had been renamed Olympia Brewing Co. when this photo was taken in 1911. The imposing new brewhouse was built in 1906.

of his beloved wife Johanna in 1911, had taken ill. He gave up the Tumwater house to live in his Hotel Leopold at Bellingham. On September 24th, the old master brewer suffered a heart attack and died in his suite.

Soon after this, on November 3rd, a second tragedy struck Olympia Brewing when the people of Washington, Oregon, and Idaho voted to prohibit the manufacture and sale of alcoholic beverages, including beer.

With the death of its founder and the voting in of prohibition, the happy life at Olympia Brewing Co. came to an end. After his father's death, Peter Schmidt was elected president of the firm, and his first sad task was to plan to phase out the company his father had worked so hard to build. The law allowed one year for breweries to sell their inventories, but brewing stopped at once.

Prohibition in Washington took effect on January 1, 1916. Peter Schmidt and his brothers, Frank and Adolph, and the other officers of the company decided to keep the Tumwater and Salem plants open by producing nonalcoholic beverages. The main brewery at Tumwater began making "Fruju" fruit drinks, chiefly an apple beverage called "Applju." The plant in Salem made a loganberry product called "Loju."

Five to ten tons of apples were pressed each day at the Tumwater plant, and "Applju," as well as jellies and jams, were sent to American forces during World War I and to markets nationwide.

Another Prohibition business the company entered into was ice and cold storage. The Olympia Dairy Products Co., headed by Adolph Schmidt, furnished cold storage for eggs and dairy products, using the former brewery equipment.

But the fruit drink business proved economically unsound, and in October 1921, on the 25th anniversary of the Olympia Brewing Co., the doors were closed to wait out the long dry spell that had fallen over the nation.

The Schmidt family, meanwhile, looked to other business interests besides ice and cold storage, including hotels, creameries, and freight companies.

With Repeal in 1933 came a new beginning for Peter and Adolph Schmidt. Funded by a successful stock offer, the brothers began construction of an immense modern brewery just up the hill from the old site.

The first batch of Olympia Beer was ready for market on

This 22-ounce Olympia Beer bottle was one of the first to come off the line in 1934 after repeal of Prohibition.

January 14, 1934, accompanied by this announcement: "Today the skill of Leopold Schmidt lives again in Olympia Beer—You will welcome the good news that Olympia Beer, famous in days gone by for its supreme quality, is once again available in its original form—fully aged—brewed exactly as it was before prohibition and, as before, by the same family. Olympia Beer has always been outstanding among American Beers and old-timers will remember its golden goodness, the secret of which is the subterranean spring water, discovered at Tumwater in 1895 by Leopold Schmidt, founder of the Olympia Brewing Company."

Total production for 1934 was 75,000 barrels. The new brewery employed 112 men, over half of whom were Olympia Brewing employees before Prohibition. Peter Schmidt was president,

Adolph was vice president, and Frank Kenney, creator of the "It's the Water" slogan in 1902, was made secretary-treasurer.

Success and growth of the post-Prohibition Olympia Brewing Co. was immediate, and soon twelve gigantic storage tanks were built.

Through the lean years of World War II, with its restrictions and beer shortages, the company was under continual change and modernization. In full production again following the war, Olympia was the first West Coast brewery to use stainless steel beer kegs for their entire operation. Olympia Beer was first sold in cans in 1950, and by the end of 1951 the annual brewing output reached 672,844 barrels.

Adolph Schmidt had passed away in 1947, and in 1953 Peter retired as president. Adolph's son, Adolph "Bump" Schmidt, Jr., who had helped reestablish the brewery in 1933, was made president and carried on the 58-year Schmidt family tradition. With constant expansion under Adolph Jr.'s guidance, beer production in 1956 hit one million barrels for the first time in company history.

On October 31, 1963, "Bump" Schmidt stepped down because of illness and Robert A. Schmidt was elected president by the board of directors. "Bump" passed away the next year, ending 31 years of service to the family business.

In 1974 a new era evolved at Olympia Brewing when Leopold F. "Rick" Schmidt, at age 34, was elected president of the company. A great-grandson of the founder, Rick prepared to take Olympia to new heights. Throughout its 80-year history, Olympia had produced one beer, but shortly after Rick Schmidt began his tenure as president, the company acquired the Theodore Hamm Co. of St. Paul, Minnesota for $22 million. Then, in 1976, the Lone Star Brewing Co. of San Antonio, Texas was purchased.

From a one-label company brewing only Olympia Beer, the Schmidt family business owned three major breweries and seven brands of beer by the mid-70s. And by 1979 Olympia had its brands marketed in thirty states. Also in that year, the company made a highly successful entrance into the light-beer market with "Oly Gold."

But the winds of change blow in unexpected directions in today's complex brewing industry, and in 1982 the Pabst Brewing Company bought Olympia and its holdings. Then in 1985, Paul

Kalmanovitz and his General Brewing Co. purchased the Pabst Company and now owns Olympia.

Today's brands brewed at the Olympia plant in Tumwater include "Olympia," "Olympia Gold," "Olympia Light," "Hamm's," "Hamm's Special Light," "Buckhorn," "Pabst Blue Ribbon," and "Olde English '800' " (a Pabst label). In addition, General Brewing's old favorite, "Lucky Lager," is produced at Tumwater, as are two Stroh's brands, under contract to that company.

The beer is brewed in a gigantic 24,000-gallon brewkettle and two 12,000-gallon brewkettles. The packaging department fills 1,260 bottles and 2,050 cans of beer each minute.

The Olympia Brewery welcomes visitors, and tours are conducted from 8 a.m. to 4:30 p.m. every day except Thanksgiving, Christmas, and New Year's. The venerable old 1906 brewhouse is nearby and can be viewed up close or from Interstate 5.

Over nearly a century, the little family brewery at Tumwater Falls has evolved into an empire that Leopold Schmidt never could have imagined on that day in 1895 when a barber told him about the good local water.

Interlude Two

"Belly Up to the Bar, Boys": The Saloons

"There is nothing which has yet been contrived by man, by which so much happiness is produced as by a good tavern."

—*Samuel Johnson*

SALOONS WERE A NEIGHBORHOOD social institution in the old days. Often they were the principal public places of rest and entertainment for men, where townsman and stranger met for the common exchanges of life. There they discussed politics and weather and troubles and travels. There, standing with one boot on the bar-rail or slumped comfortably in a chair, a man could find a few moments of quiet or friendly talk over a cool glass of beer.

And because most of the beer in the old days was consumed in these drinking emporiums, they deserve a nostalgic place in this story of the Pacific Northwest brewing industry.

Hollywood Westerns notwithstanding, much more beer than whiskey was downed in saloons. Except for certain arid regions of the Southwest, where it was impractical to import beer from distant breweries, kegs and bottles of ice-cooled beer were an integral part of the barroom inventory.

In the Pacific Northwest there was not a single district where the foamy refreshment could not be found. Even the most remote mining and lumber camps of Oregon and Washington had local beers available, and often Eastern ones too. Whenever freight wagons or rails brought goods to a Northwest community, in the loads would be sloshing wooden kegs or rattling bottles. Some

The old-time saloon was a relaxation and social center.

saloons, in fact, served nothing but beer. They were called beer parlors or beer gardens and were usually run by Germans, sometimes retired brewers.

Before Prohibition, the saloon was strictly a male stronghold. With the exception of those ladies known at the time as "pretty waiter girls," and others of the "soiled dove" persuasion, the local barroom was a males-only proposition. Again, contrary to many Western movies, most of the old-style thirst-parlors were rather tame places, where the business at hand was sipping, talking, and at most a friendly game of cards. Occasionally an eruption took place, of course, and in some of the lower-class, cramped, dimly-lit establishments, known as "deadfalls," violent debates arose more frequently. But in the great preponderance of saloons and taverns a man could indeed expect to have a quiet, congenial time at the cost of 5¢ a beer.

Behind the stand-up bar (stools were strictly a post-Prohibition notion) was commonly found an ornate backbar, centered with a large, elegant gilt-edged mirror. Many of these furnishings came around the Horn from cities in the East or Europe. Lining the backbar were shelves of bottles and gleaming glassware, and a

In the new mining and logging camps of the Pacific Northwest, saloons were often thrown together quickly and offered few amenities. Notice the gun in a beer glass on the bar.

variety of murals, nude paintings, beer advertisements, sporting prints, and lithographs adorned the walls, all directed at pleasing the male clientele.

And tucked away under the bar, snug and cool in beds of ice, were bottles and wooden kegs of the brewers' finest products. Beer was drawn from the kegs by simple or ornate brass pressure taps on the bar, or by a gravity faucet inserted directly in the keg.

Over it all presided the aproned saloonkeeper, ever watchful for empty glasses and mugs. Like the barber, he was much more than a businessman. He kept the pulse of the community; he was friend, confidant, nurse, and advisor to his customers. The best ones knew when to brighten the proceedings with a fund of good humor and tall tales, and they knew when to minister to a patron's emotional needs. The man who ran a popular saloon was the brewers' best customer.

The Tradition of the "Free Lunch"

In the August 7, 1886 edition of The Dalles *Mountaineer* was this advertisement, common to the times:

—Grand Opening of the ORO FINO SALOON—
Celebrated Columbia Beer on draught—5¢ a glass
Also, Gambrinus Bottle Beer
Special Rates to Families
A Splendid Free Lunch for customers

It is not certain where the institution of the free lunch originated. Some students of the subject believe it started among the saloons of San Francisco's Barbary Coast. Others say it began in the Exchange Bar in New Orleans, where after paying for two drinks, customers could help themselves to smoked oysters, barbecued pork, and gumbo. Wherever it originated, the free saloon lunch became a hallowed tradition in the West.

This is the way it worked. The customer first had to buy a 5¢ beer. After paying for his beer, he was then welcome to go to the free lunch tables and help himself from the offerings. If he was a

Businessmen get together over sociable glasses of beer in a 1905 Baker, Oregon drinking emporium.

regular customer of the saloon, he might be able to select his food first, take it to a table, and then buy his beer. But no freeloader needed apply. The procedure was based on the honor system, and any ne'er-do-well who thought to avail himself of the free lunch without buying a beer was quickly given the bum's rush out the door.

In truth, the free lunch tables, bountiful though most were, had the effect of bringing on a powerful thirst. The food was usually spicy and salty—fresh fruit, vegetables, or salads were never a part of the old-time free lunch. The lunch tables featured such items as sausages, slabs of roast beef and ham, giant dill pickles, smoked herring, kettles of pickled fish, loaves of bread, and wheels of cheese. Bowls of hot, spicy stew were sometimes available in Pacific Northwest saloons during winter, and the lunch tables always had large pots of mustard. If the customer was not particularly thirsty before lunch, he certainly was afterwards.

One of the most famous free lunches in the Northwest could be found at the widely known Erickson's Place in Portland. From the 1880s until prohibition, August Erickson was the undisputed king of Portland saloonkeepers. His immense saloon, also known as the Workingman's Club, boasted the "longest bar in the world," though other saloons in other towns laid claim to having longer ones. But there is no doubt that the bar at Erickson's was very long and very busy.

The building that housed Erickson's took up most of a city block on West Burnside Street. There were five doors opening out onto three different streets, and its five great bars wound around and through the big building for a total length of 684 feet. The saloon was lavishly furnished with the best of everything, including a concert stage and a large pipe organ. The bars, fixtures, and mirrors were worth a fortune. There were elegant, classic nude paintings, and on one wall a gigantic mural, entitled "The Slave Market," depicted the auction of Roman captives.

August Erickson catered primarily to laboring men—loggers, miners, sailors, and the hundreds of teamsters, longshoremen, and railroad workers of Portland and the Northwest. The Workingman's Club was crowded, noisy, and happy.

The rule at Erickson's was "large drinks at a low price." Hard liquor went at the bargain price of two shots for a quarter, and beer was sold in big 16-ounce schooners for 5¢.

Bartenders and customers gather outside for a photograph at Keane's Saloon in Tacoma. The two men on the right are carrying beer pails.

While Gus Erickson was generous with his drinks, they could not compare with his idea of a free lunch. His lunch tables were jammed with great platters of thick-sliced ham and roast beef. A wide variety of cheeses, sausages, and smoked fish—including salmon—were on the lunch bar, and their aromas wafted through the place. Large jars of pickles and brined sardel (a small sardine-like fish) were always present, as were huge plates of stacked bread—sliced exactly one-and-a-half inches thick. On the free lunch counters were quart pots of mustard so hot it took a full schooner of beer to quell the fire.

This magnificent, bounteous repast, available for the price of one 5¢ beer, was advertised by Erickson as his "Dainty Free Lunch."

With rare exceptions, the old-time saloon is gone. Who can say that their contributions were not as noteworthy, in their way, as those of other frontier institutions. In any case, the early-day prominence of the saloon earned for it an appeal and customer loyalty that Prohibitionists found deeply frustrating.

And during that long-gone era, with its 5¢ beers and free lunches, the saloons were the brewers' best customers.

Chapter Six

In the Old Style: The Microbreweries

EVERY BEER WAS AS individual as the brewmaster who made it, in the years before Prohibition. In the old days a strong thirst would send a man down to the corner saloon, often with a tin pail in one hand, for some cool lager drawn fresh from the tap. Most likely it was made at a nearby brewery, which in some cases was right on the premises. The beer was distinctive—rich in malts, hops, and character.

Then came Prohibition and the Depression, wiping out nearly all the Pacific Northwest breweries. A handful carried on, but by the end of World War II most local beer was poured from just a few corporate kettles. The beer was still good, but for the most part it had lost the individual identity that made each old-time brew unique.

Then, starting in the early 1980s, a disparate group of entrepreneurs, nostalgic beer lovers with business smarts, started opening small commercial beer-making concerns known as microbreweries. Now the Pacific Northwest has a concentration of microbreweries unmatched anywhere in the country.

The microbrewery has brought much of the old-style brewing tradition full circle. Many of the microbreweries today have an attached saloon, as in olden times, and most sell their product only by the keg, as did early breweries before bottling became common. Some of the microbreweries are now bottling their beers, and all of them maintain their individual flavorful identities and brewing recipes, just as the pioneer German brewers did in the last century. The number of microbreweries is growing each year, attended by a large and faithful following.

These are the present Pacific Northwest microbreweries. Any or all are worth a visit.

OREGON MICROBREWERIES

Bayfront Brewery & Public House

748 SW Bay Blvd.
Newport, OR 97365
(503) 265-3188

Bayfront Brewery opened in July 1989 on Newport's historic waterfront. This brewery is companion to the Rogue Brewery in Ashland. Brewmaster John Maier uses Oregon hops and barley to produce "full-bodied ale with a lot of character."

Available in kegs, bottles, and at the brewery's Public House are: Rogue Olde Crustacean, Mogul Madness, Waterfront Lager, Golden Coast, New Porter, Shakespeare Stout, and Rogue Smoke (Welkommen).

BridgePort Brewing Company

1313 NW Marshall
Portland, OR 97209
(503) 241-7179

Established in 1984, BridgePort is Oregon's oldest operating microbrewery. Owners Dick and Nancy Ponzi expanded their brewing facilities in 1987 to meet increased demand, and still maintain their high quality.

The brewery now makes BridgePort Ale, Coho Pacific Light Ale, Blue Heron Pale Ale, and Double Stout. Blue Heron and Coho Pacific are bottled and available throughout the year. A specialty brew is Old Knucklehead Barleywine. Experimental brews are served at the pub.

BridgePort Brewing Company's Blue Heron Pale Ale
received a gold medal for package design in the
1990 National Paperboard Packaging Competition.
Also shown is Old Knucklehead Barleywine, a specialty brew.

Cornelius Pass Roadhouse
Sunset Highway & Cornelius Pass Road
Route 5, Box 340
Hillsboro, OR 97123
(503) 640-6174

Opened in 1986 on the site of the Imbrie Farmstead, the Cornelius Pass Roadhouse resides in a country mansion that was built in 1866. The country setting adds charm to this McMenamin brewery.

The Roadhouse brews house ales, such as Crimson and Maid Marion, and they also serve the other popular McMenamin ales, which include Cascade Head, Crystal, Ruby, Terminator, and Hammerhead.

Deschutes Brewery & Public House

1044 Bond Street
Bend, OR 97701
(503) 382-9242

Located east of the Cascades in central Oregon, the Deschutes Brewery was established in 1988. Head brewer John Harris chiefly uses four different varieties of Oregon hops in the brewing process.

Cascade Golden Ale, Bachelor Bitter, and Black Butte Porter are the house brews, available year-round. A seasonal brew is also offered and may feature: Jubelale, Mirror Pond Pale Ale, Bond Street Brown Ale, or Simtustus Weissbock.

Fulton Pub & Brewery

0618 SW Nebraska
Portland, OR 97201
(503) 246-9530

The large outdoor beer garden at this McMenamin brewery is crowded with a wide array of flowers and hops. Fulton Pub & Brewery opened in May 1988, and Fulton Ale was developed as the house specialty. They also serve the familiar McMenamin ales.

Highland Pub & Brewery

4225 SW 182nd
Gresham, OR 97030
(503) 665-3015

Using fermentation tanks purchased from the Whitbread Brewery in London, England, Highland began brewing in June 1988. At the opening celebration of this McMenamin brewery, the mayor of Gresham had the honor of pouring the first ale.

They offer Cascade Head Ale, Crystal Ale (named for the old Crystal Ballroom in Portland), Terminator, Hammerhead, and Ruby Ales.

High Street Brewery & Cafe

1243 High Street
Eugene, OR 97401
(503) 345-4905

A turn-of-the-century dwelling has been home to the High Street Brewery since November of 1988. An old-fashioned brick-lined beer garden is a charming addition to this McMenamin brewery and cafe. The brewing equipment is located in the basement, where High Ale was developed.

Manager Jennifer Gomez says the most popular beer is Terminator Stout, with Ruby Tuesday as the next choice. Besides these, a nice variety of other microbrewery beers is offered, as well as the McMenamin line of ales.

Hillsdale Brewery & Public House

1505 SW Sunset Blvd.
Portland, OR 97201
(503) 246-3938

Hillsdale Brewery was the first in the McMenamin chain founded by Mike and Brian McMenamin. As of April 1990, the McMenamins have opened seven other brewpubs in Oregon. Wanting time to develop "a native product, not a British ale, nor a German ale," they encourage experimentation and have established their own niche among Northwest beer lovers.

Five of their most popular ales are: Ruby, Terminator, Hammerhead, Crystal, and Cascade Head.

Hood River Brewing Company

506 Columbia Street
Cannery Square
Hood River, OR 97031
(503) 386-2247

Opened in the fall of 1986, Hood River Brewing is located in the former Diamond Fruit Cannery at the newly landscaped and

The familiar Full Sail logo of Hood River Brewing has come to mean excellence to Northwest beer lovers.

renovated Cannery Square. For visitors to the brewery and White Cap BrewPub a self-guided tour is available.

Brewmaster James Emmerson produces a fine line of popular beers, including Full Sail Amber Ale, Full Sail Golden Ale, Full Sail Brown Ale, and the seasonal Wassail Ale.

Lighthouse BrewPub
4157 N Highway 101
Suite 300
Lincoln City, OR 97367
(503) 994-7238

Located near Cascade Head in Lincoln City, the Lighthouse BrewPub opened in July 1986. This McMenamin brewery developed Cascade Head Ale, with a hint of Oregon Hallertauer hops, and they also brew a well-received seasonal Bock.

While viewing their copper and brass mash tun and brewkettle, a wide selection of McMenamin ales can be enjoyed.

McMenamins
6179 SW Murray Blvd.
Beaverton, OR 97005
(503) 644-4562

McMenamins, which opened in April 1990, is the first brewpub in Beaverton, and also the newest brewery in the McMenamin chain. They offer a brewery tour and a wide selection of ales. Among the favorites are Crystal Ale, Hammerhead, Terminator, Cascade Head Ale, and the fruit ales, such as Ruby.

Oregon Trail Brewery
341 SW Second
Corvallis, OR 97330
(503) 758-3527

Established in July 1987, Oregon Trail Brewery is the Willamette Valley's oldest microbrewery. Brewing in a three-tier building, brewmaster Jerry Shadomy uses a copper kettle and combines multiple barleys and Northwest hops to obtain complex flavors in traditional ales.

Seasonal offerings plus three standards are available at the brewery. Extra Stout XX is brewed with Chinook and Tettnanger hops. Oregon Trail Porter blends several barleys in a unique dark ale. And Oregon Trail Ale, they say, is "Good at either end of the Trail."

The Pizza Deli & Brewery
249 N Redwood Highway
Cave Junction, OR 97523
(503) 592-3556

Owners Jerry and Bertha Miller added a brewery in July 1990 to their popular establishment. Brewer Hubert Smith uses British pale malt in brewing both pale and mild British Ales. The brewery also has a porter and special Oktoberfest brew, and plans to expand its offerings.

Portland Brewing Company
1339 NW Flanders
Portland, OR 97209
(503) 222-7150

This microbrewery was founded in January 1986 by Art Larrance (manager) and Fred Bowman (brewmaster) near the site of Arnold Blitz's original Portland Brewing Company. Their annual capacity is 7,000 barrels.

Current brews are Portland Ale, Timberline Classic Ale, and Oregon Dry Beer. They also make three selections under license to Bert Grant of Yakima Brewing—Grant's Scottish Ale, Grant's Imperial Stout, and Grant's Winter Ale.

Portland Porter and Portland Ale are available in bottles.

The quart-size Portland Porter is reminiscent of the average bottle of beer in the 1880s and '90s. Portland Brewing's smaller bottle of Portland Ale is a more common size today.

Roger's Zoo
2037 Sherman
North Bend, OR 97459
(503) 756-1463

Located in a 1920s-style building, owner-brewer Roger Scott opened Roger's Zoo in January 1987. It is the only brewery on the southern Oregon coast. Both Coos Bay Porter and North Bend Ale are brewed in fifteen- to twenty-gallon batches. Brewmaster Scott uses Cascade, Tettnanger, and Chinook hops.

Rogue Brewery & Public House
31B Water Street
Ashland, OR 97520
(503) 488-5061

Rogue Brewery & Public House opened in 1988. Located off the Plaza in Ashland on Ashland Creek, it was described by *Pacific Northwest* magazine as "perhaps America's most beautiful brewery site." Newport's Bay Front Brewery is Rogue's sister brewery.

Rogue beers available are Rogue Micro Light, Rogue New Porter, Rogue Golden Ale, Rogue Logger Ale, and Rogue Old Shakespeare Stout. Seasonal ales are also brewed, including the popular Rogue-N-Berry.

Rogue Old Shakespeare Stout, Rogue Golden Ale, and Rogue New Porter are among their bottled products.

These 22-ounce bottles from Ashland's Rogue Brewery are easily recognized by the label's cavalier, who is hoisting a frothy tankard of ale.

Steelhead Brewery
199 5th (corner of Pearl)
Eugene, OR 97401
(503) 686-BREW

Steelhead Brewery, the newest microbrewery in the Willamette Valley, opened in January 1991. Visitors can view the brewery through a large window behind the bar in the brewpub. The brewery was custom-designed in the newly constructed Station Square Building, near the Fifth Street Public Market. It offers three standard brews and a fourth specialty brewmaster's choice.

Brewmaster Teri Fahrendorf's first beer was an India Pale Ale, followed by Emerald Irish Ale for St. Patrick's Day. Other specialties include Black Pete's Porter, a ginger-flavored ale, a blackberry porter, and other house brews.

Thompson's Brewery & Public House

3575 Liberty Road South
Salem, OR 97302
(503) 363-7286

Salem's first brewpub opened in January 1990. Brewer Bart Hance developed Thompson Knek (a dark cherry ale), which is served as the house ale at this McMenamin brewery. Manager Randy Turner notes that they brew fifteen to twenty barrels per week.

In addition to their house ale, Thompson's offers the full line of McMenamin ales.

Widmer Brewing Company

929 N Russell
Portland, OR 97227
(503) 281-BIER

The Widmer family opened their brewery in 1985 with a distinctive group of top-fermented German-style beers. Brewmaster Kurt Widmer traveled to Düsseldorf to learn about *Altbier* (old beer) at Zum Ürige, a prestigious brewing plant.

Widmer's now occupies the adjacent brick Smithson (circa 1890) and McKay (circa 1893) Buildings, both of which are on the National Register of Historic Places.

Beers available in kegs from Widmer are Widmer Alt, Widmer Weizen, Widmer Festbier, Widmer Märzen, Widmer Bock, Widmer Hefeweizen, and Oktoberfest; occasionally other specialties are brewed.

Widmer Brewing Company

923 SW Ninth
Portland, OR 97205
(503) 221-0631

Widmer Brewing Company expanded in August 1990 to this second location, where brewer Frank Commanday brews the popular Widmer Weizen and Widmer Hefeweizen.

WASHINGTON MICROBREWERIES

Big Time Brewing Company

4133 University Way NE
Seattle, WA 98105
(206) 545-4509

Owner Reid Martin opened Big Time Brewing Company in the University District on December 1, 1988. Big Time's pub is patterned after a turn-of-the-century saloon, with an eighty-year-old bar. Brewery tours and a collection of antique beer memorabilia add to the enjoyment of beer brewed in the old style.

Always on tap at Big Time are Prime Time Pale Ale, Atlas Amber Ale, and Cool Creek Porter. Brewmaster Ed Tringali has developed a fine group of specialty beers, which include Watertown Wheat, All Out Stout, Slam Dunkel Weizen Bock, Bhagwan's Best India Pale Ale, Old Wooly Barleywine Ale, and Julefest, a Christmas ale.

Duwamps Cafe & Seattle Brewing Company

301 Queen Anne Avenue N
Seattle, WA 98109
(206) 281-8200

Duwamps Cafe & Seattle Brewing Company owners Susan Benz and Phil Rogers have created a charming setting reminiscent of European cafés. Tables on the awning-covered terrace look across to Seattle's Space Needle, while the upstairs lounge and dining room have a view of Puget Sound and the peaks of the Olympics. The brew house is visible from most seating areas.

Owner-brewer Phil Rogers poured his first batch in November 1990. Seattle Brewing offers Pier 86 Pale Ale, Raven's Dark Lager, Sockeye Ale, and a brewer's seasonal.

Fort Spokane Brewery
W 401 Spokane Falls Blvd.
Spokane, WA 99201
(509) 838-3809

Located in a 100-year-old hotel, the Fort Spokane Brewery has a spacious pub overlooking the brew house. James Bockemuehl, president of the brewery, is a direct descendant of Bernard Bockemuehl, who owned the Fort Spokane Brewery in Miles, Washington from 1887 to 1906. The microbrewery tapped its first beer in July 1989.

Brewer John Eyre offers an interesting assortment of brews, including Ben's Special Bitter, Border Run Ale, Red Alt, and Bull Dog Stout. There are also seasonal specials, such as an Oktoberfest brew and Godzilla Dry for April Fool's Day in 1990.

Hale's Ales
E 5634 Commerce
Spokane, WA 99212
(509) 534-7553

First established in Colville in the winter of 1983 by owner-brewer Mike Hale, this microbrewery carried on the town's brewing tradition started in 1865 by John Hofstetter. Brewmaster Hale uses a distinctive yeast strain from Norwich, England in his brewing. The brewery was moved to Spokane in September 1991.

Always available are Cascade Mist, Pale Ale, Special Bitter, Celebration Porter, and Moss Bay Amber Ale. Several specialty brews are produced during the year. The old favorites are Irish Ale, Harvest Ale, and Wee Heavy Holiday Ale.

Hale's Ales
109 Central Way
Kirkland, WA 98033
(206) 827-4359

Hale's Ales in Kirkland is the second brewery opened by owner-brewer Mike Hale. Since early 1987, he and his assistant, Phil

O'Brien, have brewed the same high-quality products found at the original brewery.

Year-round offerings include Cascade Mist, Pale Ale, Special Bitter, Celebration Porter, and Moss Bay Amber Ale. Among their seasonal specialties are Harvest Ale, Irish Ale, and Wee Heavy Holiday Ale.

Hart Brewing
110 W Marine Drive
Kalama, WA 98625
(206) 673-2121

Open since 1984, Hart Brewing has moved to a new, larger location in Kalama. The building is glass-enclosed on three sides and gives an excellent look at their brewing plant. Owner and general manager Jack Bryce and brewmasters Clay Biberdorf and Jerry Bockmore continue to produce a fine selection.

Brewed on the banks of the Columbia River, using a water source that originates in the glacial areas of Mount St. Helens, their familiar bottled brews are Pyramid Wheaten Ale, Pacific Crest Ale, Pyramid Pale Ale, Sphinx Stout, and Snowcap Ale.

Hart Brewing's top-fermented ales rank high among Northwest favorites.

Maritime Pacific Brewing Company
1514 NW Leary Way
Seattle, WA 98107
(206) 782-6181

Situated in the Ballard district near Salmon Bay, Maritime Pacific Brewing is housed in a brick building with ornamental iron on the windows and large double doors. Owner George Havcock and brewer Larry Rock produced their first batch of Flagship Red Ale, a German *Altbier,* in Septemper 1990. Maritime's Christmas 1990 seasonal was Navigator Dark Ale, and other seasonals are planned.

Noggins Brewery and Restaurant
400 Pine Street
No. 352
Seattle, WA 98101
(206) 682-BREW

Noggins Brewery and Restaurant opened on October 20, 1988, and is located in Westlake Center. Brewmaster Craig Skelton introduces a wide array of beers, with a rotation of five or six selections available at one time.

Noggins' diverse offerings include Special Old Bitter, Noggins Pale Ale, India Pale Ale, Dark Ale, Scottish Ale, Autumn Alt, Barleywine, Weizen Bräu, Dunkel Weizen, Hefeweizen, Porter, Stout, and Lagers.

The Pacific Northwest Brewing Company
322 Occidental Avenue S
Seattle, WA 98104
(206) 621-7002

Located in Seattle's historic Pioneer Square, the Pacific Northwest Brewing Company produced its first beer in May 1989. The large windows, sidewalk seating, gleaming tanks, and warm woods create a pleasant setting for the visitor.

Brewmaster Ken Brusco has developed the following assortment of beers served on the premises: Blond, Bitter, Gold, Amber, Stout, and Winter Bräu. Six guest beers are also available, offering a wide selection.

Pike Place Brewery
1432 Western Avenue
Seattle, WA 98101
(206) 622-1880

Nestled in the heart of the Pike Place Public Market, owner Charles Finkel opened Pike Place Brewery in October 1989 with a never-to-be-forgotten parade led by brewmaster John Farias. Seven types of Northern Brewer Hop vines in oak barrels mark the brewery site in the Market. Their copper kettle was custom-built for Pike Place Brewery, and the brewkettle's warm glow invites the visitor inside.

Head brewer John Farias and assistant head brewer Jason Parker produce Pike Place Ale, in kegs and bottles, and for their 1990 seasonal Christmas brew introduced XXX Stout.

Redhook Ale Brewery
3400 Phinney Avenue N
Seattle, WA 98103
(206) 548-8000

Owners Paul Shipman (president) and Gordon Bowker (vice president) held the Redhook Ale Brewery grand opening in 1982. When increased demand for Redhook brews made a move to larger quarters necessary, Shipman and Bowker chose the historic Fremont Trolley Car Barn. Brewing in the newly designed Redhook Ale Brewery began in September 1988. The Trolleyman Pub offers specialty beers and popular Redhook standards, along with delicious snacks in a smoke-free environment.

Brewmaster Al Triplett oversees a brewing team that creates a wide variety of traditional brews. Available on draft or in bottles are Redhook Ale, Redhook ESB, Blackhook Porter, Wheathook,

Winterhook Christmas Ale, and Ballard Bitter, with its label featuring Captain Ballard and the familiar slogan, "Ya Sure, Ya Betcha."

Redhook Ale Brewery honors Seattle's historic trolleymen on their top label. Pictured here are three of their best-known brews.

Roslyn Brewing Company

33 Pennsylvania Avenue
Roslyn, WA 98941
(509) 649-2232

Roslyn Brewing Company is one of Washington's newest microbreweries. Opened in May 1990, the brewery is a family operation, with brewer Dino Enrico, Lea Enrico Beardsley as business manager, and her husband Roger in charge of marketing.

Their initial brew is Roslyn Beer, a lager using local ingredients—Roslyn water from the high Cascades, Yakima Valley hops, and Palouse malt.

Thomas Kemper Brewery

22381 Foss Road NE
Poulsbo, WA 98370
(206) 697-1446

Thomas Kemper Brewery, established in January 1985, was founded by partners Will Kemper and Andy Thomas, with daily business now conducted by general manager Bob Breslauer. The brewery is located in the former Foss Meat Packing building on 3½ acres in a peaceful country setting near Poulsbo.

Brewmaster Rande Reed oversees production of their line of beers, including Thomas Kemper Helles Lager, Thomas Kemper Dunkel Lager, and Pilsner. Seasonal favorites are Oktoberfest, Winter Bräu, and Bock.

Three of the Thomas Kemper fine line of beers are available in bottles for enjoyment at home.

The familiar, well-designed bottles of Bert Grant's
Yakima Brewing & Malting Company.

Yakima Brewing & Malting Company
32 N Front Street
Yakima, WA 98901
(509) 575-1900

Opened in July 1982, Yakima Brewing & Malting Company is housed in the historic Opera House, the same quarters occupied by the turn-of-the-century brewery, North Yakima Brewing & Malting Company.

Owner-brewer Bert Grant has crafted a fine selection of keg and bottled beers, which have a faithful Northwest following. They include Grant's Scottish Ale, Grant's Imperial Stout, Grant's India Pale Ale, Grant's Weis Beer, Grant's Celtic Ale, and Yakima Spiced Ale.

The advent of the Pacific Northwest microbreweries has brought a nostalgic turn to the beer industry. They are today's answer to the local pioneer brewer, who did his best with modest facilities to satisfy a thirsty populace.

Brewing by hand in the best traditions of their long-gone predecessors—Saxer, Kopp, Schmeig, Zweifelhofer, Rast, Stahl, Grathwohl, Schutz, Hofstetter, and all the rest—the artful brewers of today do indeed complete the circle of Pacific Northwest brewing history.

Glossary

Adjuncts. Materials such as rice or corn that are used in beer-making, other than malted barley, to add body or alcohol to the beer.

Ale. A beer fermented with a yeast that works throughout the beer, including the top, and does not settle to the bottom. Ale is very pale in color; it originated in England in the 15th century.

Artesian. Pure, crystal-clear water produced by natural springs or deep wells, which is forced up by underground pressure.

Barley. The prime ingredient of beer. After its conversion to malt, it provides the body and substance of the beer.

Barrel. Most of the pioneer brewers put up their beer in 5-, 10-, and 15-gallon kegs. Larger 31-gallon barrels were also commonly used for bigger shipments, and that is the size referred to in annual production records. Hogshead casks (63 gallons) were sometimes used for storage and shipping by rail or steamship. Modern beer barrels, still 31 gallons, are made of stainless steel or aluminum. Today's small picnic or pony barrel holds exactly 3.875 gallons.

Beer. Beer is the generic term for all malt beverages produced by the fermentation process, including ale, porter, lager, and stout. The principal difference between ale and lager (the type of beer generally consumed in the United States) is in the fermentation process. (See under individual types of beer.)

Bock. A dark brown lager beer with a strong hop taste. It originated in the German city of Einbeck, whose name was confused with *ein Bock,* the German name for goat, and the beer unfortunately became known as *bock* or *goat beer.*

Bräumeister. The German word meaning "brewmaster."

Brewkettle. A large pear- or dome-shaped vessel—usually of copper—used for boiling hops and wort to extract the hop-resins and flavor in the brewing process.

Brewmaster. The "master chef" of beer brewing. In early times a brewer earned the title by graduation from a brewer's academy at one of the great German brewing capitals. Later, excellent brewer's schools were established in America.

Cooper. A person whose work is making or repairing barrels or casks. Many breweries had a cooperage on the premises, and some small ones contracted with the village cooper.

Cream ale. A beer fermented with a top-fermenting yeast. It has a very pale color, a mild hop flavor, and is flavored with vanilla.

Fermentation. The stage in the brewing process when yeast is added to the wort (a procedure known as "pitching the wort"). The yeast converts the starch to sugar, producing alcohol and carbonic acid gas (the effervescence in beer).

Hops. A perennial plant of the nettle family. Grown extensively in the Pacific Northwest, the ripened cones of the hop plant are dried and used to impart flavor and preservative value to beer.

Lager. A light-colored beer, fermented with a "bottom yeast" that settles to the bottom of the fermenting tank. Its name comes from the German word *lagern* (to store), because lager beer is aged before being placed on the market. Lager is what most Americans think of when they mention beer.

Malt. Germinated barley that has been dried and ground; used as a chief ingredient in making beer.

Malt liquor. A variety of lager with a higher alcoholic content.

Mash. A mixture of crushed malt grains and hot water, which is extracted from the mash tun as liquid mash, or wort.

Mash tun. A tun is a large cask or vat. The mash tun is where the malt is mixed with hot water to form a grist known as mash. From the mash tun the strained liquid runs into the brewkettle.

Pilsener. A very light lager beer with a medium hop flavor. Most of the beer made in North America was a type of Pilsener.

Porter. An English-style dark ale, usually strong, but not as strong as stout.

Stout. An English-style dark malt liquor with a strong malt flavor, sweet but tart in taste.

Weissbier. A top-fermented, pale-colored beer (*weiss* is German for "white") made mostly from wheat and a limited amount of barley malt. It has a strong hop flavor.

Wort (pronounced *wert*). The solution of malt extract (mash) in water, derived from the grist in the mash tun. The malt extract and hops are boiled together in the brewkettle to form wort. The wort is then cooled and pitched with yeast to start fermentation. After fermentation has been completed, the wort is known as beer.

Yeast. The microorganism fermenting agent that transforms wort to beer by turning the wort sugars into alcohol and carbonic acid gas.

Source Notes

There has never been a book written on the history of the Pacific Northwest brewing industry. A number of books have been published on beer in general, and some of these, listed in the Bibliography, were helpful to us as sources of information on certain historical aspects of the brewing business.

The information on specific breweries came chiefly from primary sources, such as: historical records of the United States Brewers' Association; contemporary newspaper accounts; business directories; county and state records; and the myriad of letters, documents, reminiscences, and advertisements concerning old-time local breweries found in the archives of 54 county and regional historical societies.

Much local brewery information was also found in state and local histories and profiles of noteworthy residents, most of which were written around the turn of the century or before, when the breweries were still in existence.

The photographs came primarily from regional historical societies and private collections. All the modern views of existing and former brewery sites were taken by the authors.

Bibliography

Books

Abel, Bob. *The Book of Beer.* Chicago: Henry Regnery Co., 1976.

Allen, Frederick Lewis. *Only Yesterday.* New York: Harper & Row, 1931.

Bagby, Clarence B. *History of Seattle.* Chicago: S. J. Clarke Publishing Co., 1916.

Bonney, W. P. *History of Pierce County, Washington.* Chicago: The Historical Publishing Co., 1927.

Chapman Publishing Co. *Portrait and Biographical Records of Western Oregon.* Chicago: Chapman Publishing Co., 1904 (no author cited).

Clallam County Historical Society. *Jimmy Come Lately.* Port Angeles, Washington: Clallam County Historical Society, 1971.

Clark, Norman H. *The Dry Years: Prohibition and Social Change in Washington.* Seattle: University of Washington Press, 1965.

Clarke Publishing Co. *History of the City of Spokane and Spokane County, Washington.* Chicago: S. J. Clarke Publishing Co., 1912 (no author cited).

Clarke Publishing Co. *History of the Yakima Valley, Washington.* Chicago: S. J. Clarke Publishing Co., 1919 (no author cited).

Colvin, D. Lee. *Prohibition in the United States.* New York: Doran & Co., 1926.

Cottone, Vince. *Good Beer Guide.* Seattle: Homestead Book Co., 1986.

Dodge, Orvil. *Pioneer History of Coos and Curry Counties.* Salem, Oregon: Coos-Curry Pioneer and Historical Association, 1898.

Douglas County Historical Society. *Historic Douglas County, Oregon.* Dallas, Texas: Taylor Publishing Co., 1982.

Edwards, Jonathan. *An Illustrated History of Spokane County.* Spokane: W. H. Lever, Publisher, 1900.

Fagan, David B. *History of Benton County, Oregon.* Portland: A. G. Walling Co., 1885.

Gaston, Joseph. *The Centennial History of Oregon.* Chicago: S. J. Clarke Publishing Co., 1912.

Gilbert, Frank T. *Historic Sketches of Walla Walla, Whitman, Columbia and Garfield Counties, Washington Territory.* Portland: A. G. Walling Co., 1882.

Grant County Museum. *The History of Grant County, Oregon.* Dallas, Texas: Taylor Publishing Co., 1983.

Hines, H. K. *An Illustrated History of the State of Oregon.* Chicago: The Lewis Publishing Co., 1893.

Hunt, Herbert. *Tacoma: Its History and Its Builders.* Chicago: S. J. Clarke Publishing Co., 1916.

Interstate Publishing Co. *An Illustrated History of Klickitat, Yakima and Kittitas Counties.* Seattle: Interstate Publishing Co., 1904.

Klamath County Historical Society. *History of Klamath County, Oregon.* Dallas, Texas: Taylor Publishing Co., 1984.

Lewis Publishing Co. *A Volume of Memories and Genealogy of Representative Citizens of the City of Seattle and County of King, Washington.* Chicago: The Lewis Publishing Co., 1903 (no author cited).

Martin, Paul J. *Port Angeles: A History.* Port Angeles, Washington: Peninsula Publishing Co., 1983.

Mullen, F. C. *The Land of Linn.* Albany, Oregon: Privately published, 1971.

Munsey, Cecil. *Collecting Bottles.* New York: Hawthorne Books, 1970.

Parsons, Col. William. *An Illustrated History of Umatilla County.* Spokane: W. H. Lever, Publisher, 1902.

Peterson, Emil & Powers, Alfred. *A Century of Coos and Curry.* Portland: Binfords & Mort, Publishers, 1952.

Prosser, Col. William F. *A History of the Puget Sound Country.* New York: The Lewis Publishing Co., 1903.

Salem, Frederick W. *Beer, Its History and Economic Value as a National Beverage.* New York: Arno Press, 1972.

Seattle Historical Society. *Seattle Century—1852–1952.* Seattle: Superior Publishing Co., 1952.

Shiach, W. S. *An Illustrated History of Morrow County.* Spokane: W. H. Lever, Publisher, 1902.

Siebel, Dr. John E. & Schwarz, Anton. *History of the Brewing Industry and Science in America.* Chicago: Privately published, 1933.

Sinclair, Andrew. *Prohibition: The Era of Excess.* New York: Little, Brown & Co., 1962.

Spencer, Lloyd. *A History of the State of Washington.* New York: The American Historical Society, 1937.

Trade & Commerce Publishing Co. *Review of the Industries of Walla Walla.* Walla Walla, Washington: Trade & Commerce Publishing Co., 1891.

Van Syckle, Edward. *The River Pioneers: Early Days on Gray's Harbor.* Seattle: Pacific Search Press, 1982.

Walling, A. G. *Illustrated History of Lane County.* Portland: A. G. Walling Co., 1884.

Walling, A. G. *Illustrated History of Southern Oregon.* Portland: A. G. Walling Co., 1884.

Wallerstein Co. *Forty Years A-Brewing.* New York: Wallerstein Co., 1950.

Western Historical Publishing Co. *An Illustrated History of Baker, Grant, Malheur and Harney Counties.* Chicago: Western Historical Publishing Co., 1902 (no author cited).

Western Historical Publishing Co. *An Illustrated History of Central Oregon.* Spokane: Western Historical Publishing Co., 1905 (no author cited).

Western Historical Publishing Co. *An Illustrated History of Stevens, Ferry, Okanogan, and Chelan Counties.* Chicago: Western Historical Publishing Co., 1904 (no author cited).

Western Historical Publishing Co. *An Illustrated History of Union and Wallowa Counties.* Chicago: Western Historical Publishing Co., 1902 (no author cited).

Newspapers, Oregon

Albany – *Democrat-Herald.*

Astoria – *Daily Astorian.*

Baker – *Bedrock Democrat.*

Burns – *Harney County News.*

Canyon City – *Blue Mountain Eagle.*

Coos Bay – *Times.*

Eugene – *Guard; Register-Guard.*
Grants Pass – *The Courier.*
Heppner – *Gazette.*
Jacksonville – *Democratic Times; Oregon Intelligencer; Oregon Sentinel.*
Marshfield – *Sun.*
Medford – *Mail-Tribune.*
Oregon City – *Enterprise.*
Portland – *Bulletin; Oregon Journal; The Oregonian.*
Roseburg – *Plaindealer; Review; Umpqua Ensign; Western Star.*
Salem – *The Oregon Statesman.*
Sumpter – *Blue Mountain American.*
The Dalles – *The Dalles Mountaineer.*
Union – *Eastern Oregon Republican.*

Newspapers, Washington

Aberdeen – *Herald.*
Bellingham – *Herald.*
Chelan – *Chelan Valley Mirror.*
Colfax – *Palouse Gazette.*
Colville – *Republican; Index.*
Ellensburg – *Capital.*
Kittitas – *Standard.*
Olympia – *Washington Standard; Olympian.*
Port Angeles – *Olympic-Leader.*
Port Orchard – *Independent.*
Port Townsend – *Leader.*
Roslyn – *Roslyn Sentinel.*
Seattle – *Post-Intelligencer; Seattle Times.*
Spokane – *Chronicle; Spokesman-Review.*
Tacoma – *Tacoma News; News-Tribune.*
Vancouver – *Columbian.*
Walla Walla – *Washington Statesman; Union.*
Yakima – *Herald.*

Periodicals

Brewers Digest; Modern Brewery Age; Old Bottle Magazine; Oregon Historical Quarterly; Pacific Northwest Quarterly; The Coast; The New Brewer.

About the Authors

Gary and Gloria Meier are Pacific Northwest history researchers and writers. Both were born in California and share a lifelong interest in West Coast history. Museum and library work during college days furthered their interest in historical research. They are currently active in fifteen Pacific Northwest historical societies and are members of the Western Writers of America.

The Meiers specialize in original research on Pacific Northwest subjects that have not previously been dealt with at book length. They have published four books on a diverse range of topics: *Knights of the Whip: Stagecoach Days in Oregon*; *Those Naughty Ladies of the Old Northwest*; *Whitewater Mailmen: The Story of the Rogue River Mail Boats*; and *Brewed in the Pacific Northwest.* Their historical articles have appeared extensively in numerous regional and national publications.

Gary and Gloria live with two cats on the Willamette River in Eugene, Oregon, where they are working on their next book.

Index

This book was set in 10-point Baskerville at Fjord Press,
with chapter opening caps in Floradora.

Cover design by Jane Fleming, using Old Lace Xenotype,
Stationers Semi-Script, Copperplate Gothic Bold,
and Egyptienne F. Bold Condensed 67.

Coming in 1992

Brewed in California
by Gary & Gloria Meier

A lively account of the more than 450 historic breweries that have operated in California, including an up-to-date list of all the new microbreweries. Watch for it, but please don't order before June.

Other titles in Fjord's Western Writers Series

No. 1

Riding the High Country

by Patrick T. "Tommy" Tucker

151 pages, $8.95 trade paperback

This is Tommy Tucker's account of his friendship with Charles M. Russell, the cowboy artist, during Russell's first years on the Montana range. These outrageous escapades, and this last glimpse of a time when Indian and cowboy coexisted, are told in the colorful lingo of the 1880s.

"For anyone who enjoys cowboy yarns and tall tales, this book . . . is a treasure trove."
Publishers Weekly

"The author . . . takes the reader on the dusty cattle drive on the range where cowboys bathed when they happened to be near water, drank whiskey *in case* they ran into rattlers, and stayed long in one place only when they died."
Tom Griffith, *The Rapid City Journal*

"These well-told tales will acquaint you with the bachelor Russell in a new way. If you . . . like the humor of understatement, or collect delightful idioms, you will have fun with this book. The fast-paced tales will entertain young and old alike."
Mac Swan, *The Missoulian*

No. 2

Woodsmen of the West

by Martin Allerdale Grainger

With an Afterword by Murray Morgan

199 pages, $8.95 trade paperback

Grainger takes us back to the days of seven-foot saws, donkey engines, and double-bitted swamper's axes. The rain was endless, the boats were held together with baling wire, and the work was perilous. The book also exposes the ruthless cut-and-run logging practices prevalent in the Northwest in the early 20th century.

"This engaging firsthand account of handlogging along the north coast of British Columbia at the turn of the century evokes both the flavor of an era long vanished and timeless observations on human nature . . . The astute insights Grainger lends to his encounters, along with color and humor, capture a dramatic period in western Canadian timberland."
Publishers Weekly